# JUST A SMALL TOWN SOUTHERN BOY

Larry W Bowen

Published by Hemingway Publishers

Cover design by Hemingway Publishers

ISBN: Printed in the United States

# PREFACE

It is my hope that this book of my life and growing up in the 1950's, 60's, and 70's in the South—without a father and raised by a loving grandmother—can show you that you can overcome life's adversities. I want this story to be more than just memories on a page. I want it to reach into your heart, to show that you can grow to love all people, to believe in the good that still lives in the world, and to understand that God reads the heart—not the color of your skin.

I share these memories as they live inside me—unpolished, sometimes painful, often tender, and always real. Life wasn't easy, and sometimes it wasn't fair, but through it all, love—real, deep, tough Southern love—was there.

ENJOY

# TABLE OF CONTENT

# Chapter 1
# 1956: A Year That Changed Everything

Life in the South in the 1950s moved at a slower, gentler rhythm. Dirt roads crunched under the weight of old Fords and mule-drawn wagons. Kids played barefoot until their feet turned black from the dust, and porch swings creaked in the humid air while cicadas sang lullabies to the night.

Of course, I was not born yet. But the world I was born into had already started rumbling beneath the surface. My mother was just fifteen when she got pregnant. That kind of thing—back then, in the deeply religious and socially rigid communities of the South—wasn't just frowned upon. It was seen as a scandal.

In those days, you were hidden. Whispers moved faster than the wind, and judgment hung in the air heavier than humidity in July. Families did whatever it took to protect their name and hush the shame.

My grandmother and grandpa—from everything I was later told—went absolutely nuts when they found out. My grandmother, a church-going woman with a backbone forged from fire and faith, couldn't

1

comprehend what her baby girl had done. My grandpa, well, he was more fire than faith. He could cuss for five minutes straight without repeating himself, and when the news came down, the air in that small farmhouse turned electric.

My mother was hidden away like a secret nobody wanted to admit existed. For months, she stayed in that house, blinds drawn, barely stepping outside. And on Christmas Eve of 1956, during one of the heaviest snows the town had seen in years, her water broke.

The snow was knee-deep, thick and silent, blanketing the entire southern farm community in white silence. It should have been peaceful, even beautiful. But inside our house, it was chaos. The roads were shut down. Christmas lights blinked on empty streets, and the little hospital nearby—a brand-new building—was practically deserted. No nurses on duty. No doctor.

That's when my grandpa, thinking fast, remembered a man he knew from his bootlegging days—a guy with a rugged old Jeep that could handle the snow like a plow through molasses. That man came, wheels crunching across the white, headlights slicing through the storm. He drove my terrified, shivering, teenage mother to the hospital.

From what I've been told, they had to call in a doctor who was off duty, probably warm at home, sipping something strong in front of a fire. And from all accounts, he was not happy about being pulled from his cozy holiday to deliver a baby that nobody even wanted to admit was coming.

But I came anyway.

I popped out into this strange, frozen world. I imagine my cry must have echoed through those empty hospital halls like a siren announcing something new had arrived—a life not planned, not expected, but definitely not silent.

My mother held me, barely more than a child herself. I've often tried to picture what she must have felt in that moment. Love? Fear? Regret? Maybe all of it wrapped together in a tight knot she didn't know how to untangle.

The next morning, while the rest of the town was opening presents and carving hams, my mother and I returned home. But it wasn't a joyous homecoming. The house felt confused. Cold. Not from the snow, but from the tension that lived in every corner.

She was scared. Fifteen years old with a brand-new baby. Still a kid, with the weight of a world she didn't know how to carry now resting in her arms.

Now, you're probably wondering where the daddy was. The truth is, no one knew for sure if he even knew I had been born. But in small Southern towns, secrets have a hard time staying hidden. And word traveled like wildfire: "Betty had her baby last night."

A few days later, my father—just eighteen himself—showed up at my grandparents' front porch. Maybe he came out of guilt. Maybe curiosity. Maybe love. I'll never know.

But I do know what happened when he knocked.

My mother, hearing that knock, must've known who it was. Maybe her heart leapt. Maybe it cracked. But she never made it to the door.

Jake Bowen—my grandpa—answered it. And Jake didn't let that boy get a foot across the threshold. See, Jake wasn't just any old Southern man. He was known all across the county. Why? Because he was a bootlegger. The kind you didn't cross unless you wanted trouble. Everybody who drank knew Jake Bowen. And they respected him—or feared him. Sometimes both.

Jake stood in the doorway, staring at the boy who had gotten his daughter pregnant. And in his hand, he held a claw hammer.

"You turn around right now," Jake said, his voice a thunderclap. "And you don't ever set foot on this porch again."

And that boy did exactly what he was told.

He turned. He left. And he never came back.

Looking back now, I don't even blame him. I mean, would you have come back if Jake Bowen told you not to? Not with that hammer in his hand. Not with fire in his eyes.

So that was that. That was my beginning. My mother, my grandmother, my grandpa—and no father in sight.

I never laid eyes on my real dad until decades later, in the 1980s. By then, it was too late to know him. But that story comes later.

For now, this is how my life began—on a snowy Christmas Eve, in a town that whispered, in a house that trembled with new truths, with a mother who was barely grown, and a hammer-wielding grandfather who made sure the past stayed outside the door.

# CHAPTER 2
# A YOUNG MOM'S LIFE

My mother was very young—sixteen years old, barely more than a child herself—and scared to death of what lay ahead for her with a baby boy while she was still in school. I can only imagine her sitting there in that tiny kitchen, elbows resting on a faded oilcloth table, staring into space, trying to figure out how her life had shifted so suddenly. The world must've felt heavy, pressing on her shoulders like a sack full of stones, weighing her down so she couldn't breathe or see clearly past tomorrow.

Of course, my grandparents were still in shock, too. A lot of unanswered questions would come up soon, and answers wouldn't come easy or quick. My grandparents weren't rich—no, they were poor people just trying to survive. They knew more about struggling than comfort. My grandma worked a midnight shift in a cotton mill, her small frame hunched over machines that whirred loudly through the night, cotton dust thick in the air, clinging to her hair and clothes. That was the primary work back in the '50s, and people didn't complain—at least not openly. They just kept moving, kept enduring because survival left no room for anything else.

My grandpa Jake was a womanizer and loved to get around. He was the kind of man women noticed. Handsome as a movie star from one of those black-and-white films down at the local theater, he had dark hair always slicked back, eyes sparkling with mischief. He loved to wear bib overalls with starched white shirts beneath them—shirts my grandma meticulously cleaned and ironed, though she knew exactly where he'd been and who he'd been with. She probably pressed down on those shirts a little harder when anger flared up inside her. But she never said much about it, never threw his clothes out on the porch, just kept starching those white shirts like it was her sacred duty or silent protest.

My mother had tough decisions ahead—what would she do for me? With my grandparents already stretched thin, their own worries piling up like logs stacked high for winter, my mother decided, painfully, that she had no choice but to send me into foster care. That was no easy decision for her, I'm sure. It must've felt like tearing away a piece of her own heart, but circumstances gave her no choice.

The courts took me away and placed me in a foster home with a lady by the name of Ms. Angel. Of course, I was just a baby and didn't have a clue about what would come next.

My mother quit school and continued her life, though she still liked to get around out in the world. She probably did it trying to feel some freedom again, chasing a little relief from her guilt and sorrow. The judge had told my mother clearly: "When you can prove you can provide a stable home life, you may get your son back."

As I look back on that, it feels almost impossible. How does a sixteen-year-old girl get a stable home life? At that age, stability seemed as distant and unreachable as the moon.

It broke my grandmother's heart when I went away to Ms. Angel's home. She carried that grief quietly, locked deep inside her chest like a heavy secret she couldn't bear to share. But I learned later in life that Ms. Angel was a good person. She held me close, rocked me through long nights when I cried, fed me from warm bottles, and made sure I was cared for and safe until life would turn again.

# CHAPTER 3
# MY GRANDMOTHER AND
# GRANDPA–THEIR LIFE

My grandma was born in 1899 in Davie County, North Carolina, a rural farm community where the soil was hard, and the life even harder. My grandpa was born not too far away, in Farmingtown, NC, in 1895. I really don't know how they met, but it probably happened at some church social or a barn dance where fiddles played lively tunes beneath flickering kerosene lanterns. They married young, probably drawn to each other by laughter and hope, never imagining the trials waiting down the road.

Eventually, they had fourteen children, my mother being the last—the baby of the family. Fourteen mouths to feed at times when even feeding one seemed daunting. They worked hard, my grandmother especially. She worked in that nasty cotton mill on midnight shifts for thirty-five long years—how she did it, I'll never understand. Her tired feet would shuffle home before dawn, shoes coated in cotton fibers, her hands cracked and raw, only to start her second shift of cooking, cleaning, and raising those kids. Their generation was tough as leather, hardened by necessity.

She lost two children at birth and later three more as adults. She bore losses like a steady tree weathering storms. My grandmother always told me, her voice trembling slightly with emotion, "The hardest thing you will ever do is look down at one of your children in death." Her eyes, cloudy with age, always held that sadness close, a constant companion.

My grandpa Jake, meanwhile, was a bootlegger, running mountain whiskey out of the mountains of North Carolina with three of his sons. They were notorious around those parts. Even the state troopers knew Jake Bowen. My grandma told me stories with a mixture of pride and resignation about the boys getting pulled over for speeding, trucks rattling, filled to the brim with mason jars of clear, potent moonshine. The trooper, approaching slowly, would peer inside and, seeing their familiar faces, always asked the same question:

"Y'all Jake's boys?"

"Yes, sir!" they'd answer, grinning sheepishly, eyes sparkling just like their father's.

"Well," the trooper would sigh, tipping his hat back with a knowing smile, "have a nice day—and slow down next time!"

Looking back, I guess my grandpa kept the troopers supplied pretty well with mountain white, creating something akin to a small-town Southern mafia, just friendlier and less organized. Back in those days, it was a different culture; everybody knew everybody for miles, and business was done with a nod, a handshake, and a quiet understanding.

Life went on for my grandparents, tough as ever. They worked endlessly, tended a sprawling garden, and canned vegetables for winter. Some of that food went to my grandpa's produce market downtown, where he made pretty good money, selling tomatoes and squash alongside his liquor bottles hidden beneath burlap sacks.

Of course, my grandparents hadn't forgotten about me. They visited when they could, holding me tenderly, speaking softly, promising that soon they'd bring me home. Their goal, from the moment I'd left, was to get me out of foster care, and several months later, their prayers were finally answered.

I was about six months old when the courts approved for me to go home to my grandparents, and oh, were they happy. My mother still wasn't together yet, still searching for herself in a world that was too big and confusing, but she was there to see me come home—and at the time, that's all that mattered.

# CHAPTER 4
# LIFE CHANGES QUICK AGAIN

After six months, I went home to my grandparents, returning to a time filled with uncertainty. My mother was happy to get me home to my family, smiling wide, hugging me close as if to hold tighter this time, afraid I might slip away again.

My mom loved me, I'm sure, but being young, she was very confused—pulled in too many directions, still caught somewhere between childhood and womanhood, neither place offering her comfort or clear answers. But we carried on until she was dealt a new problem—and yep, you guessed it, she was pregnant again. Now what?!

Of course, I was just a baby; I had no clue what was happening. All I knew was warmth, laughter, and tears—adults bustling around me like worried hens, voices raised, filled with worry or disbelief. My grandparents, of course, went nuts. My grandmother, from what I was told later in life, simply couldn't believe it. She probably sank down in her rocking chair, face buried in her hands, silently shaking her head, wondering how this could've happened again so soon.

My grandpa, Jake Bowen, was out to find out who got his daughter pregnant again, pacing back and forth on the porch like a caged animal. Jake was a proud man, protective of his family, and this news spread through town quicker than a summer storm. Needless to say, Jake Bowen was going crazy, and everyone in this small town was buzzing, speculating loudly in barber shops, beauty parlors, and front porches about who the father of this one could possibly be.

Come to find out, my mother had met a man who was in the service and had a relationship with him. He was probably just another young man, his hair freshly cut short, uniform crisp, offering promises he couldn't keep. But he went away to a foreign country to serve, leaving behind no clue that he had gotten my mom pregnant. This world gets crazier as we go on.

In February 1958, on the 18th, my half-sister was born. Little did she know what she was in for, born into a world already spinning fast, a family unsure of how to handle the troubles already at hand, much less another hungry mouth.

Right after my sister was born, my grandpa had a heart attack and died. I was a little over one year old, just old enough to sense loss but not old enough to understand it. So I really never got to know my grandpa, at least not in the ways I wished I could've. But later in life, my grandmother told me stories about me and my grandpa, stories that filled gaps in my memory, bringing him back to life in small ways that meant everything to me.

One of my memories my grandmother told me was that every afternoon when he would come in from the day, he would grab me up into his strong arms and walk to the country store. It was probably one of those stores with a screen door that squeaked loudly and slammed shut with a bang behind you, candy jars lined neatly on wooden shelves. He would get me a big banana, bright yellow and ripe, and I would carry it proudly home. My grandpa would carry me, and I would wave that big banana around like a trophy as we walked up the road. To this day, I wish I had a picture of that—my tiny hand clutching that fruit, safe and happy in his arms. I guess that's why I eat a banana every morning when I get up, keeping his memory alive in the simplest way. My grandmother told me after my grandpa died, all I would say for a while was "banana, banana, banana," like a prayer or a lament.

# CHAPTER 5
# MY MOM-WHAT NEXT

My grandmother did not know what she was going to do next. She had my mom, me, and now my newborn sister all leaning on her. She was still working the midnight shift at the cotton mill, coming home exhausted with cotton lint stuck in her hair, barely enough energy left to keep us clothed and fed. All the family was frantic, arguing at the kitchen table, wondering how, in God's name, they were going to manage this time.

As my grandmother continued to provide the best she could for the family, my mom still had not gotten her act together. She drifted in and out, lost between youthful rebellion and motherly responsibility, caught up in her own struggles and unable to settle down. My grandmother couldn't keep the pace up anymore. So enters child welfare once again, bringing both help and heartache.

They helped as much as they could, but the painful decision came again—to put us back in foster care. The courts sent my sister and me to another home, fortunately together. My grandmother was adamant, fiercely demanding we not be split apart; she knew we'd need each other more than ever. A family finally agreed to take us in together— Mr. and Mrs. Smith, as my grandmother had told me later in life.

# JUST A SMALL TOWN SOUTHERN BOY

Being in a strange home is not good for young children, but we got through it somehow. My sister was a year younger than me, so she was new to this game. I'd done been in a home before, though, as an infant, and I hadn't understood much of what was going on. Now, as I approached four years old, things were clearer. I remember the first day clearly—big house, manicured lawn, the Smith kids watching us curiously, as though we were visitors from another planet.

The Smiths had two children of their own—a boy and a girl. Their home was nice; I thought they were rich, with plush couches and shiny floors, though they were just middle class. Still, to me, they seemed well-to-do considering where I came from—where "rich" meant having meat on the table every day or new shoes every year.

Their kids were older than myself and my sister and pretty spoiled from my standard of living. At this time, my sister was two, and I was three, close to four years old. Their kids were probably eight and ten. They had everything—bicycles, toys, clothes without patches or stains. I was shocked kids lived like that.

We were not treated as well as their own kids when it came to basic things. We were not abused, just little differences kids notice deeply. Like when it came to eating dinner and breakfast—their kids would eat fried chicken or pork chops for dinner, while we got fried bologna or something not as good as what they had. Of course, still to this day in my life I love fried bologna—HA HA!

Some nights, we would go to bed hungry. In the quiet darkness, I'd hear my sister softly crying in her bedroom, hunger gnawing at her tiny belly. I'd get up, tiptoeing down creaky stairs, heart pounding in fear of being caught, to steal cookies or crackers or whatever I could quietly grab. I'd sneak back upstairs to her room, and I could still see her eyes lighting up in the moonlight when she saw the motherload of goods I brought. She'd eat till she wasn't hungry, and then she'd do something strange—like a squirrel, she hid the rest under her mattress for later when hunger returned. After she was satisfied, I'd slip back to bed. I wouldn't hide food, but my sister always would, her quiet way of feeling safe.

When I tell people about this later in life, they find it amazing that really happened. Foster care in the '50s and '60s was not all champagne and strawberries, though few outside ever knew it.

I could not wait for visitation time when my mom and grandmother would come visit. We'd sit by that big picture window in the living room, faces pressed against glass, watching and waiting to see them drive up, hearts racing in excitement. How exciting it was to see them—we wanted to go home terribly to a place we truly belonged.

My grandmother would always bring us a toy or a new set of clothes, simple things that filled us with joy. My sister and I would cry for hours when our mom and grandma would leave, tears soaking our pillows. But we knew they'd be back in a month, bringing us hope again.

Life continued on in foster care, our dreams sustained by those short visits, holding on to hope that one day, we'd go home for good.

# CHAPTER 6

Life with a Different FamilyFall was quickly coming, a slow creep of cooler air that whispered against the windowpanes, leaves turning from deep green to fiery shades of amber and crimson, and a new season settling in. School was starting back for the kids—shiny new shoes, crisp backpacks, their voices bouncing through the hallways each morning as they grabbed their lunches and disappeared out the door. But for us, we stayed home, lingering like shadows in the corners of a house that didn't quite feel like ours. We didn't do a whole lot while their kids were in school. Mostly, we just stayed in the house, drifting from room to room, killing time in that peculiar stillness.

They didn't act like we were even there. Not in a mean way, not with any harsh words or cruel looks—just with a kind of quiet, a comfortable ignoring, like we were pieces of furniture they'd grown used to, blending into the background. My sister usually spent her days staring out the window, her small fingers tracing invisible patterns on the glass, her eyes wide and searching, waiting. Waiting for Mama to come back, for Grandma's familiar face, for anything that would mean we weren't forgotten.

The holidays were approaching, and the house transformed almost overnight. They threw themselves into Christmas like it was some grand, magical festival. Strings of sparkling lights twisted around the banister, wreaths of pine and ribbon hung on the doors, and the smell of cinnamon and pine needles filled the air. They had a beautiful tree—a towering green giant, so tall it brushed the ceiling, dripping with ornaments that shimmered like tiny treasures. Silver tinsel caught the light, and a golden angel perched at the very top, her wings spread wide. I stood there, staring at it, my breath catching in my throat. I had never seen anything like it. To me, it was like looking at the White House itself—grand, glowing, something out of a dream.

But beneath all that beauty, I began to notice something else— something that gnawed at me in a way I didn't quite understand then. They loved their children very much—anyone could see that. Their faces lit up when their kids came into the room; their laughter was warm and full. But when it came to us, that warmth was...muted, distant. We were there, but we weren't part of it. I look back now and understand why. We were a meal ticket. I hate to say it, but in my heart, that was true. We didn't bring joy; we brought a check. They didn't treat us the same, and a quiet, bitter jealousy began to simmer in me, though I didn't have the words for it then.

I really don't even remember their children's names to this day, and to be honest, I don't really care. Faces blurred, names faded, but the feeling stayed. As the days rolled on in that foster home, nothing really changed—day in, day out, the same cold kindness, the same food, the same quiet ache that we carried like a hidden bruise. Life was just...crappy, to put it plain. Just a long, gray stretch of waiting— for Mama, for Grandma, for someone to walk through that door and take us home. We never really understood why we were there. I didn't know what we'd done wrong, why we'd been left behind, but I knew what it felt like. It felt like floating in a space that wasn't yours, a balloon without a string.

But we survived. We carried on, even when the weight of it seemed too much for little shoulders.

# Chapter 7
# Holidays Arrive in
# Our Foster Home

The Smiths had everything decorated so beautifully that even now, I can still see it—lights twinkling like stars on a winter's night, the tree's green branches heavy with ornaments, each one shining like a little jewel. As a kid who had never seen anything like it, it was overwhelming. I felt like I was staring at the White House, like I'd wandered into some grand, glittering palace. I had never seen so many presents piled beneath a tree in my short lifetime—boxes wrapped in bright reds, shimmering golds, and deep greens, each with a ribbon tied in a perfect bow.

At night, when the house had gone quiet, my sister and I would sneak downstairs, our bare feet silent on the cold wooden floors. We would creep close to that towering tree, the smell of fresh pine filling the air, our tiny hands reaching out to gently touch the gifts, our fingers brushing against the tags. We checked, again and again, searching for our names—but they were never there. Not one tag with "To" followed by our names. My sister's face would fall a little, but she'd force a smile, telling me not to worry. "Mama and Grandma will bring us something," she'd whisper, her voice steady, like she was trying to make it true just by saying it. And I'd nod, because I wanted to believe it too.

A few days before Christmas, I overheard the Smiths talking. They'd bought their boy something for Christmas, something big, and it was hidden in the garage. My ears perked up like a hound's, and my heart thudded with a mix of excitement and something else—curiosity, envy, maybe just the need to feel like a part of something, even if only by knowing the secret.

That night at dinner, Mr. Smith looked at us with that stern, no-nonsense look of his. "Nobody goes in the garage," he said, his voice flat and firm. "Not until after Christmas." My sister and I nodded, but I couldn't help the flicker of wonder that burned in my chest. What could it be? What could be so special, so hidden away?

The next day, the house was quiet—too quiet. Mr. Smith was outside working in the yard, raking leaves in the crisp air. His wife was in the kitchen, and their kids were off doing whatever it was they did. My sister was upstairs, playing in her room. And the garage...the garage was right there.

I don't know what took over me, but I felt pulled, a tug in my chest that wouldn't let go. I slipped out the back door, the cold air biting at my cheeks, and I crept around the side of the house. The garage door wasn't locked. It groaned a little as I pushed it open, and the smell of oil and sawdust washed over me. And there it was—the brightest red go-kart I had ever seen, gleaming under the dim light like something out of a dream.

My eyes went wide, my heart pounding. Without thinking, I climbed into the seat, my small hands gripping the steering wheel. For a moment, I wasn't just a boy in a cold garage—I was flying, racing, free. I laughed out loud, my voice bouncing off the garage walls.

Then—BAM—the garage door roared open, flooding the room with blinding light. Mr. Smith's shadow stretched long, and his voice crashed over me like a thunderclap.

"GET OFF THAT GO-KART NOW!" he roared, his face twisted in anger. I stumbled out, my small legs shaking. His voice was a storm, harsh and furious, words I'd never heard before spilling from his mouth. "Get to your room! Don't come out until I say so!"

I ran, tears burning hot in my eyes, my chest tight. I threw myself onto my bed, burying my face in the pillow, sobbing, trying to drown out his voice still ringing in my ears. My sister came in, her gentle hands on my back, her voice soft and soothing. "Brother, it'll be alright. You'll have one one day."

But I didn't believe her.

I'm sixty-seven years old now, and every time I see something red, a car, a toy—it pulls me back. Funny how a moment can brand you, how a spark of joy turned to shame can follow you all your life. I never did get a go-kart. But I sure do buy a lot of red cars.

# CHAPTER 8
# CHRISTMAS DAY ARRIVES

Christmas arrived with a soft hush over the house, like the world itself was holding its breath. The sky was a pale, wintry blue, and the air felt different—charged with the kind of magic that only Christmas morning can bring. My sister and I woke up early, eyes bright, hearts thumping, because today wasn't just any day. Today was Christmas. Today was the day we would see Mama and Grandma.

We didn't need an alarm. The excitement was enough to drag us out of bed while the sky was still streaked with dawn. We shuffled to the big picture window, the one that overlooked the gravel driveway, and pressed our faces against the cold glass, waiting. We didn't move much, just sat there, knees pulled up, sharing that quiet, hopeful energy that only kids can summon. We kept glancing at each other, sharing small smiles and little whispers about what they might bring us, what stories Mama might tell, how Grandma might smell like biscuits and lavender.

Time seemed to stretch like taffy. Hours passed, but it didn't matter. We stayed put, eyes glued to the road. Finally, around noon, a familiar old car came rumbling up the drive, backfiring and coughing like it always did. Our hearts leapt, and in an instant, we were up and running. The sound of the car's engine was like the song of salvation, and we tore through the front door, not even bothering to grab our coats. The cold bit at our cheeks, but we didn't feel it.

My sister was squealing, her little feet kicking up loose gravel as she dashed ahead of me. It was a miracle to us, seeing Mama step out of that car, her coat too thin for the weather, but her smile warm and bright. Grandma came next, slower, but with that same gentle, familiar presence that always made me feel safe. My sister reached them first, throwing herself into Mama's arms, and I followed, nearly tripping over my own feet in my hurry.

As we hugged them tight, I couldn't help but notice Mr. and Mrs. Smith standing on the porch, stiff and quiet, like they were just waiting for this to be over. It made me feel odd, like happiness wasn't allowed to stretch too far.

Mama opened the trunk, and there they were—presents, all wrapped in mismatched paper, some of it crinkled and reused, but to us, they might as well have been wrapped in gold. My sister and I were laughing and crying all at once, dragging the packages to the porch, our hands full of boxes and bags. I felt happy for my sister, seeing her so full of life and excitement. But for me, it wasn't as simple. The memory of that red go-kart still loomed in the back of my mind, heavy and stubborn like a knot I couldn't untie.

Mama noticed me lagging behind, my movements a little slower than usual. She crouched down beside me, her voice soft. "What's wrong, Larry Wayne?" That's what she always called me—never just Larry, and sometimes she'd even call me "son" when she was feeling tender. I glanced at her, trying to force a smile, but it didn't quite reach my eyes.

"Nothing, Mom. It's alright," I mumbled, looking down at the snow-dusted ground. I couldn't quite put it into words, that ache inside. I didn't want her to worry. I just wanted to go home to Grandma's house, where it was safe and familiar.

Mama patted my shoulder, a little sigh escaping her lips. "I'm working on it," she whispered. She always said that—like it was a promise, like one day it would all be better. I wanted to believe her, but there was a part of me that had learned not to hold on too tight to hopes like that.

We sat on the porch and started opening our presents, my sister tearing into hers like a wild thing, her face lighting up as she uncovered a beautiful doll with curly hair and a frilly dress. My heart lifted a little at her joy, and I let myself get caught up in it, even just for a moment.

One of my packages was heavy. The paper wrinkled around the corners. I peeled it back, and there it was—a bright red firetruck, shiny and new. I should have been thrilled, and in a way, I was. It was a good toy, sturdy and colorful. But that red...it hit me right in the chest. I couldn't explain why, but it made my stomach twist. Mama couldn't figure it out—why I wasn't grinning from ear to ear. I tried to hide it, not wanting to hurt her feelings, but I couldn't shake that pang.

We were still sorting through our presents when Mama cleared her throat, looking serious. "I have some news," she said, glancing at Grandma before turning back to us. "Your mama's met a man," she said, her voice a little hesitant, like she wasn't sure how to say it. "And we're gonna get married."

I blinked, trying to wrap my head around it. "So I'm gonna have a daddy?" The words felt strange on my tongue, like they didn't quite belong. My sister didn't really care, too caught up with her new doll, rocking it gently in her arms. She was still little, barely old enough to understand what that meant. But to me, it was big—huge, even. I couldn't help but wonder if this new man might mean we could finally leave the Smiths' house and go home.

Mama gave a hopeful smile. "Hopefully soon, I can get you kids home." But I'd learned early that life didn't always work out the way you wanted. I nodded, trying not to get too wrapped up in the idea. It sounded good—too good.

I stayed quiet after that, my thoughts running in circles. I knew better than to get my hopes too high. Life could change in an instant— I'd learned that already. So I just let it go, trying to focus on the day, on the feeling of Mama's arms around me, on the way Grandma smelled like biscuits and lavender.

We waited, like we always did, hanging on to Mama's words and hoping that this time, they'd stick.

# CHAPTER 9
# THE BIG PHONE CALL

The holidays came to a close, as they always do, leaving behind that bittersweet feeling of endings. The world seemed to spin on like it always does, with everything getting back to "normal," though what normal meant to everyone else wasn't the same for me and my sister. For us, it felt more like we were waiting for a storm to pass, unsure of whether it would bring us sunshine or something else. There were days when we just waited, barely breathing, hoping to see our mom and grandma again, praying we could leave that place. Our hopes hung on a single thread—that the red go-cart that had been the centerpiece of my torment would soon be gone, and with it, some of the misery of our lives. It was a strange feeling, thinking back now—it was like you could almost touch the chance of freedom, but it was always out of reach.

Weeks went by, and still, there was no word from our mother. We didn't know what was going on, why she wasn't calling. I'd stare at that red machine from the porch, wishing for it to disappear—wishing the same for the helplessness it represented. Then, one day, the phone rang. Mr. Smith answered it, and my sister and I froze, listening in, straining to catch anything that might give us an idea of what was happening.

We couldn't quite make sense of it. Something about court proceedings, but we didn't understand what that meant, not really. The words didn't make any sense to us then, and even the tone of the conversation didn't help clear it up. All we knew was that Mr. Smith was on the phone for a good while, about fifteen minutes or so. After that, there was silence. He hung up without saying a word, and there I was, sitting there, looking at him like he might give me the answer to a question I didn't even know how to ask. I couldn't stand it. I wanted to know—*desperately* wanted to know—what that call had been about. Why wouldn't anyone tell us?

The afternoon stretched on in a haze. I could feel the weight of the waiting, like the air was thick with it. It was almost dinner time, and part of me thought, *Maybe when we sit down to eat, they'll finally tell us.* My stomach growled at the thought of fried something, but my mind was caught on what I'd heard in that phone call. Would they let us know? Would they tell us the truth? My sister was silent, sitting beside me like she'd already made peace with the unknown.

By the time we sat down at the table, nothing had been said. No mention of the phone call, no explanation. That silence in the room felt suffocating. I couldn't hold it in anymore. I cleared my throat, feeling the courage swell up in me, my hands trembling just a little. *This is it, I told myself. I have to ask.*

"Mr. Smith," I said, my voice quiet but steady, "did my mom call today? I heard you talking about a hearing."

His eyes snapped to mine, and I could see the surprise in his face. I must've caught him off guard, but I wasn't going to back down. His gaze shifted to my sister, and I saw him frown a little, maybe wondering if we had overheard something we weren't supposed to.

28

His wife, though, was quicker on the uptake, leaning in with a nudge to him. "You might as well tell them," she said, and he relented.

He looked at us then, a long pause before he spoke. "Okay, kids, here's the deal. You're going to court next week for a hearing, to see if you're going back to your mom. Could be your grandma, too, I don't know, but either way, you're going somewhere."

I sat there, almost not believing it. The words hit me like a rush of cool air on a hot day. "You're going somewhere," he'd said. In that moment, it felt like the world opened up just for me. I didn't know what winning the lottery felt like, but this felt close—close enough that for a second, I could almost believe it.

But then he hit me with the cold water. "Don't get too excited," he warned. "It might not happen."

Just like that, the magic disappeared. The joy that had bloomed inside me deflated like a popped balloon. The reality of it all sank in. Still, I didn't care. Even that tiny bit of hope was worth it, worth the hurt that would follow if it didn't pan out. I wanted to believe it would. And so, I prayed that night, as the darkness swallowed the room and the sounds of the house settled around me. I didn't know God very well, but I knew enough to ask him for what I wanted. I didn't know the words, but I knew the feeling. *Please,* God, *take us home.*

# CHAPTER 10
# COURT DAY-WHAT'S NEXT

Time trudged on, the days slipping away like sand in an hourglass. A couple of weeks passed before Mr. Smith gave us the news. My mom had gotten married, and there was a hearing set for Monday morning, in Winston-Salem, North Carolina. We were going to court to see if we'd be going home to our mother—or to my grandmother. Truth be told, I didn't care much either way. I just wanted to *go*. But, if I'm honest, I missed my grandmother so much that it made my chest ache thinking about it. She was my rock, the one constant I could hold on to in a world that seemed to keep shifting.

The day came, and I couldn't shake the nerves. Monday morning. The trip to Winston-Salem. I didn't know much about courts, just that it was serious business, and serious business made me more scared than I cared to admit. I could feel the fear in the pit of my stomach as we made our way there. My sister and I huddled together in the backseat, clinging to each other for comfort, our hands pressed tight against each other, but neither of us dared to speak. It was like we both knew that once we crossed the threshold into that courthouse, nothing would be the same.

We arrived at the court, right around 10 AM, and the air was thick with the smell of old wood and polished floors. A lady met us as we walked in, her face polite but distant. She told us the judge would meet us soon. My mom was there, of course, along with her new husband, who was a tall man, sharply dressed. He looked nice enough, but I didn't care much for that. I wasn't thinking about him—I was thinking about my mom. I just wanted to go home, wherever that was.

And then the judge came out of his chambers. He was a big man, with a kind face, though I couldn't tell if it was kindness or just his job face. He introduced himself and the woman with us. My mom and grandmother both stood up, and I felt the room get colder with the weight of their eyes on me. The judge asked me how old I was. I froze for a moment, my nerves nearly overtaking me. But I managed to squeak out, "Four years old."

He asked my sister the same thing, but she looked at me, like she was waiting for me to answer for her. So, I did. "She's two, Judge."

The judge nodded, like he was taking it all in, then glanced at the papers in front of him. "Would you two like to come with me?" he asked.

That was it. *Would you like to come with me?* My heart skipped, my chest tightened, and I could feel my legs go shaky. But the lady beside us reassured us. "It'll be okay," she said, guiding us gently to the back of the courtroom.

In the judge's chambers, the air was calmer, quieter. He was nice—gentle, even. I remember him offering us candy, and for a brief moment, the nervousness began to slip away.

"Are you ready to go home?" he asked.

I didn't even hesitate. "YES!" I shouted, my voice so loud it startled my sister. But I didn't care. My heart felt like it was bursting with excitement. I wanted to scream again. I wanted to jump, to run, to fly out of there and never look back.

The judge told us that Mom was married now and had a stable home for us. He looked at my sister, who stayed silent, her little eyes wide, then turned to me again. "Do you have any questions?"

I didn't think for a second. "Can I go home to my grandmother?" I asked. The words felt strange coming out of my mouth, but they were honest. My grandmother was the one I wanted. The one I needed.

The judge paused. His face softened, but he asked, "Why?"

I shrugged. How do you explain that kind of love at four years old? "She's my rock," I said simply. The judge seemed to understand, but he still looked at me with that calm gaze, and he said, "Don't you think you should give your mom a chance?"

I didn't want to, but I nodded. "I guess we could try," I said, my voice small and uncertain. He reassured me that if it didn't work out, I could always go back to my grandmother.

The decision was made. We went back out to our family, still not fully understanding what had just happened, but feeling something stir inside me, something between hope and fear.

And just like that, the judge approved our return to our mother. She was overjoyed, but my grandmother's face… that was a different story. It wasn't the smile I'd been hoping for. But I didn't think about it then. I couldn't. I was too busy dreaming of what *home* might feel like now, with my mom and her new husband.

In that moment, I knew nothing about the road ahead. But I was going somewhere.

# JUST A SMALL TOWN SOUTHERN BOY

# CHAPTER 11
# A NEW LIFE, AGAIN -
# ANOTHER NEW BEGINNING

As we left that courthouse that day, I had this feeling deep in my chest, a tightness, like something was about to shift. I knew life was about to get crazy again, but I didn't quite know how or why. We were heading home with our mom, a new stepdad, and a new place to live. The change was overwhelming. Time seemed just to vanish, like one moment we were in the courtroom, and the next we were driving down unfamiliar roads, leaving behind everything that had been. Some of it was exciting, some of it was sad, and a whole lot of it just didn't make sense to me. But there was one thing I could hold onto. I wouldn't have to see that damn red go-cart again. It was a small victory, but a victory nonetheless.

Even now, years later, that red go-cart still pops into my thoughts, though I'd never admit it. Funny how the simplest things stick with you.

We pulled up to a place that, at first glance, seemed different— really different. My new dad had rented an old house on a farm pond from a man he knew. The house was, well, old. Really old. But there was something cool about it. Something that made it feel like it had stories of its own, stories that I couldn't wait to be a part of. I remember staring out the car window as we pulled up, watching catfish jump out of the water. I couldn't wait to get my hands on a fishing pole, and it felt like the pond was calling my name. Of course, my sister didn't care about that. She probably didn't even notice. But I sure did.

Mom seemed happy, and that was all that mattered at the time. To be honest, I didn't know a thing about the man she'd married, other than that he was from Iowa. He was a farmer, which I thought was kind of cool, though, at the time, I didn't have much interest in farming. I was more interested in those catfish. My new stepdad had this big field he was going to plant corn in, and he promised he'd teach me all about raising corn. I nodded, trying to sound interested, but let's be real—I was just thinking about fishing. A boy almost five years old didn't care much about crops.

As the evening came on, we finally got inside the house. They'd already set it up for us, and I was curious, eager to see what my new room would look like. It wasn't much. The house was a small cottage, but it felt like something special. I remember the floor creaking beneath my feet as I stepped inside. My room was tiny—one twin bed and a lamp. That was it. But to me, it felt like a castle. I called it my "Hilton," joking to myself. It was my space. No one was going to take it from me. I could almost hear the echo of my own thoughts as I lay there in the quiet. It was mine.

The cottage sat on about 25 acres, and the man who owned it lived right up the hill from us in a beautiful two-story house with a wraparound porch. I'd never seen anything like it before. In my little kid's mind, that man had to be rich. It was like something out of a storybook, and even though I didn't fully understand what being rich meant, I thought this man must be it. He had to be. He had everything.

That night, as I settled into bed, I felt a quiet gratitude wash over me. I closed my eyes and thanked God for everything he had done for us, especially for my sister. I wasn't sure if God even heard me then, but I knew enough to be thankful. It was something I'd always do, even if I didn't fully understand why.

When the darkness fell, the sky seemed to explode with stars. I remember staring out my window, looking up at them. They were so bright it almost felt like they were trying to say something to me. The crickets were singing, their sound so loud, it was like thunder rolling in the distance. It was beautiful, like a song, and in that moment, it felt like everything was in harmony, like the whole world was connected in a way that I couldn't explain.

It didn't take long for me to fall asleep. I remember that night like it was yesterday—the best night's sleep I'd ever had. The bed felt like a cloud, and the world outside was quiet and still. There was something about the air, something that made everything feel calm, like nothing could go wrong. I wish I could say I still lived there today, that I could go back to that peaceful place by the pond. But, knowing how things go, it's probably long gone now. Still, the memories… they'll always be with me. They're like a part of me, like the crickets' song still buzzing in my ear, like the stars still shining in the back of my mind. They never fade.

# CHAPTER 12
# A NEW SCHOOL AND
# ANOTHER BEGINNING

As we settled into our new surroundings—this strange patch of earth far from the places I'd known—it was clear we were all trying to find our footing again. For me, that meant something big: starting first grade. I remember it like it was yesterday, that mix of nervousness and excitement swirling inside my chest. My sister, though, was still too young, still wrapped up in babyhood and wide-eyed wonder. It was the first time we were going to be separated—me going off to school without her tagging along, a strange feeling neither of us had ever known.

That morning, before the sun had fully climbed high enough to light up the world, I slipped out of bed. Quiet as a mouse, I tiptoed out of the house, careful not to wake nobody. The whole world was still asleep, wrapped up in the hush of early morning, and the smell—oh Lord, that smell—of fresh dew clinging to the grass around the pond was something I couldn't get enough of. It was like breathing in a new kind of clean, the kind that washes through your lungs and makes your insides feel alive. I remember the steam rising off that pond, just like little cotton clouds, swirling slowly as the sun stretched her golden fingers across the sky. I'd never seen anything quite like it before. The whole pond was alive with morning—fish popping up to the surface for their breakfast, crickets and grasshoppers chirping their high-pitched greetings, and even the soft rustle of the trees joining in a quiet song. It felt like the pond was welcoming me into its world, telling me I was part of something bigger.

I sat there on the edge of the water, legs dangling, and breathed it all in deep. The fresh smells of the morning wrapped around me like a warm blanket, and I felt like I'd been born all over again. Right there on that damp grass, with the dew burning off under the rising sun, I knew this was the start of something brand new. I wasn't gonna waste it—not a bit of it.

Just as I was starting to soak it all in, my mom hollered from the house, "Come on, breakfast's ready!" I could hear the clatter of pans and the soft murmur of waking voices. I ran back toward the house, still feeling the cool dew squish between my toes. Out in the field, I spotted my new stepdad working—plowing a straight, narrow row with a white horse I'd never seen before. The horse moved with steady grace, muscles rippling under that shining coat, and the way my stepdad kept the lines straight as a ruler caught my attention. It was a simple thing, but at that moment, watching those perfect furrows cut through the soil, I felt a little spark of wonder. Something about that steady, measured work felt hopeful like we might just find some order in this new life after all.

My mom, she looked happy. Not just content but really happy with her new life, and seeing that made my heart swell a little. I was thrilled for her, mostly, but underneath all that, I missed my grandmother something fierce. Missed the comfort of her voice, the smell of her kitchen, the way she always had time for me and my sister. And I knew my sister missed her too, though she didn't say much about it. Still, in my heart, I had to give this a chance—for my mom's sake, even if it wasn't for mine.

Starting first grade in a new school, in a new place, with strange faces all around—that was a lot for a little boy like me. And my sister wouldn't be going to school with me, no sir. She was still too young, and that meant we'd be apart for the first time in our lives. That was hard, real hard, because up until now, we'd always been side by side. Moving around so much; jumping into strange places, it was tough on a child. But like I told myself then and remind myself now, it's all good. Just a new chapter, a new beginning, and I was ready to face it.

# CHAPTER 13
# A YEAR LATER IN MY
# LIFE NOW WHAT

I knew in my heart it was over for me. My Stepdad and mom drank a lot and fought a lot. Those fights were like storms rolling through our small house—loud, angry, and full of hurt. It seemed like every night, the drinking made them more bitter and more distant, and I just wanted it to stop. I just wanted to go home to my grandmother, where it was safe and quiet, but I knew it was out of my hands. What could a six-year-old boy do but hope for balance in a world gone sideways?

I prayed a lot for me and my sister to make a path for us to get a better life. Quiet prayers whispered into the darkness when no one was listening. I asked for a way out, for something better than what we had.

My grades were terrible in the first grade. Ms. Macy, my teacher, was always asking me, "Are you okay? You stay so quiet and displaced." She noticed the way I'd sit in the corner of the classroom like I was somewhere else, far away. But I always kept everything inside, which is not good for a child or an adult. It was like carrying a heavy secret in my chest that I couldn't share.

Later, my Mom took us to visit my grandmother, and I was so excited, always eager to see my grandmother. That house smelled like safety and home, like warm blankets and fresh bread. My mom had just been married about a year and a half—not very long at all.

As we were at my grandmother's, I heard my mom talking to my grandmother about getting a divorce from David. She wanted out. I could hear her say to my grandmother, "If I leave David, can me and my sister stay with you awhile until I get things settled?"

Of course, my grandmother said yes without hesitation. "Don't worry about Larry Wayne and Robin." They didn't see me at all when I was sneaking and listening to the conversation. I was grinning from ear to ear. *I'm going home.* I wanted to shout to the heavens.

I heard my grandmother ask my mom, "When are you going to tell the kids?" and my mom said, "Soon. They may be with you next week." Wow.

After we spent the day with my grandmother, it was time to make the trip back to the lake cabin. My mom didn't say much on the ride back. The silence was heavy, with things left unsaid. But I was busting inside to ask her what was going on. I think she knew I was aware of her life and the situation. But nobody said much going back. She just said, "Your stepdad will be out of town for a couple of weeks working in Virginia."

Inside me, I knew that was the time she was going to pack up and leave—to get out of Dodge, so to speak.

As we got home that Sunday evening, I had to get ready for school the next day. The night was quiet as we wound down to go to bed. My sister was displacent as she went to bed. She moved slow, restless like she didn't belong. I went into her bedroom and told her, "It's going to get better. Just stay patient."

As the morning progressed, getting ready to catch the bus, I was getting dressed to go to school. But for some reason, my sister didn't want me to go to school that day. She held on to me, almost like she was scared. But I told her I had to go. "I will be home soon."

So, on my way to school, I got to the bus and was out of there for a while. The school I attended was a two-story old type school, but a good school, I guess. The class was well on its way that morning. It started at 8:30 a.m. My desk was two rows from the windows.

As we were reading in class, all of a sudden, all the kids were running to the windows, hollering, "There's a little girl on a white horse in the schoolyard!"

I didn't think much of it at first, then I got a brain charge—a WHITE HORSE*!!!*

I ran to the window, knocking down my friend to get there. The teacher raised the window and started hollering at my sister. Of course, she didn't know it was my sister. My sister kept hollering, "BROTHER, BROTHER."

Everyone in the class was talking, "Who's her brother?"

I was like, "Quiet, quiet." The teacher was going to the principal's office to get my sister some help. Then I gave in, and I said, "Teacher, I'm the brother." You should have seen her face—she didn't have a clue. So she took me with her to talk to my sister.

I have to admit, she looked great on that big white horse. She was crying terribly. She just wanted her brother.

The teacher went to the principal's office to call my mom to come to school. I knew this was not going to be good.

I ran to my sister to get her off the horse. I asked her, "Why are you here?"

My sister said, "A man was going to cut her fingers off with his pocket knife, so she ran to the barn and stole the horse to get away."

I could not believe it. The horse took to her like she was meant to be there. She didn't know the horse's name, as I didn't either.

So about 30 minutes later, my mom shows up with our neighbor to help with getting the horse home. Good luck with that! Seems like the whole school was in the big front yard of the school. My sister was like a rockstar.

So now what? My mom looked lost. The neighbor said, "Robin and I will ride the horse home. You follow us in the car." I think that should be interesting.

So all the kids were cheering my sister as she rode off like the Lone Ranger.

What a day. I went back to class, dreading going home to my sister. I had no clue what my mom was going to do with her. I prayed she would get off light.

# CHAPTER 14
# MY LIFE CHANGES FOREVER
# ANOTHER BEGINNING

As a new day approached at the cabin, the kind of morning when the sun was just starting to burn off the last clinging fog, my mom came quietly into my little bedroom. The wood floor creaked under her soft steps as she stood there, looking down at me. "Larry Wayne, are you ready to go live with your grandmother?" she asked, voice low but steady.

I blinked up at her, the sunlight catching dust motes floating in the air. "FOREVER," I said without hesitation, my six-year-old heart sure as could be.

She asked, "Is that what you want?" like maybe there was room for doubt, maybe some second guessing.

But for me, there was no maybe about it. I was ready. I really didn't know how to answer fully—how could a six-year-old boy who had no real foundation in his life know? Neither did my sister. She didn't really want to go. All that change and uprooting was hard on her little heart. But I did. I knew my sister would follow me wherever I ended up, like a shadow that never left. David was long gone—I never saw him again, which was fine by me. I just wanted balance in my life, and I knew I would have that at my grandmother's house.

My grandmother didn't have much, but she was as solid as gold. She was the kind of woman you could lean on when the world was shaking. She'd worked harder than most—raising 14 kids of her own, pulling midnight shifts at the cotton mill when the world was still dark and quiet. By the time I got there, all her kids were grown and gone. So it would be me, my sister, and her. Grandma was retired now, but the strength in her hands and heart hadn't left.

When we got to my grandmother's house, we pulled up to her little rented house with a small front porch that sagged just a bit in the middle. I remember thinking, *This* is home. *My* last stop. I said a quiet prayer in my heart. The porch had a creaky swing, the kind that moved with a soft squeak. I felt a lump in my throat just looking at it.

My mom, sister, and I went inside. Grandma was all smiles and hugs, excitement shining in her eyes. Not as much as I was to see her—my heart was bursting. Mom told Grandma that the court was out of the picture for now, so the kids could stay as long as she wanted them to.

My sister didn't want to stay forever, but I did. The thought of finally settling down, even if only for a little while, was everything. Mom stayed a few hours and then left. We settled in. I had to get enrolled in another school Monday morning—new friends, new surroundings again. I was like a gypsy, always moving, never quite rooted. But I was ready to settle down again.

After three foster homes and living with my mom and her crazy husband, I didn't want no more of it. I wanted a LIFE. Something steady. Something real.

I was starting second grade, and my sister would be in first grade. Grandma had never owned a car or a house in her entire life. Born in 1899, she had a hard life, but you wouldn't guess it by the way she carried herself. She raised a big garden every year and burned coal in a little warm morning coal stove. I had never seen coal before, but I was about to learn what it meant.

My grandmother believed in chores—and boy, did she make sure we did them. My first chore was a big one. I was responsible for cutting the wood, or "kindling," as she called it, every night. On top of that, I had to carry up three five-gallon buckets of coal from the dirt basement. No light down there. I'd have to carry a flashlight with me if I didn't get it done before nightfall. That basement was deep, with old wooden steps that creaked under every footfall, making my skin crawl. The stairs groaned and whispered with every step I took down into the darkness.

Those buckets of coal were heavy for a 6-year-old, but somehow, I dragged them up the steps to the living room, careful not to spill a single piece. I put the buckets behind the stove, where the warmth would spread all through the room. Grandma kept the living room and kitchen hot and cozy, but the bedrooms and bathroom were closed off—no heat. You could see your breath in the bedrooms like it was a cold winter morning outside. And God help you if you had to sit on the commode—the porcelain was so cold your butt would stick to it. It's no joke. It would pull your skin off, and it hurt something fierce.

Grandma was making me tough, no doubt about it. My sister, though, she didn't have to do much except help in the kitchen. Grandma would let her dry a few dishes here and there. I, on the other hand, had the hard work.

Winter was still a lot to handle. Every morning, I had to shake the coal dust out of the stove and take it outside to spread over the garden. Grandma told me it was a fertilizer for the soil, though I didn't understand why then.

My bedroom was nothing fancy—just a concrete block room attached to the house. It wasn't big at all, but I had a little twin bed, and I loved it. Grandma was very thrifty and handy. She was always sewing, making curtains, and just about everything in her little house she made with her own hands.

One day, I went into my little room to see my bed and realized it didn't have a mattress. I didn't know what was on my bed at first. Grandma came in and said, "What's wrong, son?"

I said, "Grandma, what's wrong with my bed?"

She said, "Nothing, son."

"Grandma, it looks like a giant pillow on my bed."

"Well, son, it sorta is. I made it. It's a feathertick."

I said, "I can't sleep on that thing. Are you kidding me?"

Grandma said, "Get in it. You'll love it."

So I jumped in, and I disappeared inside it. I liked it so much that I almost never got out. It was amazing. Grandma said, "You'll sleep like a bug and stay warm all night." And boy, was she right—the best night's sleep I'd ever had.

That feather tick was made from quilting material and filled with duck feathers. It was like a gigantic pillow. I wish I still had it today. I was like a rat in that thing, buried so deep even the fire department couldn't find me.

Life was getting back to normal—whatever normal is. For a six-year-old, I was growing up fast.

# CHAPTER 15
# LIFE BEGINS WITH GRANDMOTHER
# A TOTALLY DIFFERENT WORLD

As I had got settled in at my grandma's, I was gettin' ready to enroll in my new school, excited and still confused—like somebody tryin' to read two maps at once. New friends to make, new rules to learn, and a brand-new world to figure out. My little suitcase was still by the bed, half-unpacked, and my Sunday shirt still smelled like mothballs and camphor. I was anxious, sure, but there was a flicker of hope in my chest. Maybe this time things would stick. Maybe this time I'd find my footing.

There was no school bus where we lived, not way out there. Just dusty roads, the smell of pine, and your own two legs. I had to walk to school—it was about two miles. A long stretch for a little boy with legs still growin' into themselves. The mornings were crisp and quiet, dew stickin' to my shoes like cold syrup, birds chattering like they had gossip to spread. But in time, I figured out the path, and it was no big deal to me. It became my trail, like I was walkin' into my own little chapter every morning.

I met a boy on the way to school who lived just a piece up the road. He had a quick kind of grin, like somebody who'd already seen more than a kid oughta, and wore his overalls like armor. We struck up a conversation, and I found out he was the same age as me and headed to the same school. That felt like a gift—somebody else walkin' the same path, both of us just tryin' to make sense of it all. He knew the shortcuts through the woods—of course he did—and naturally, I followed him.

In those days, folks didn't worry too much about little kids bein' out by themselves. The world hadn't turned mean the way it would later. The woods were thick, tangled with kudzu and blackberry vines, moss clingin' to the trunks like secrets. But this kid moved through them like Daniel Boone himself, sure-footed and fast like he'd grown up suckin' on pine bark. I followed close, slippin' on wet leaves, scratchin' my arms on branches, breathin' in the sharp green smell of sap and earth. When the weather was nice, that walk was an adventure, just two boys makin' their way. But when it rained or snowed, Lord have mercy—it was like the woods turned on us, slick and cold and full of shadows. Still, we survived. Course, I didn't tell my grandma I was cuttin' through the woods with my new friend. I figured some things was better left unsaid.

I started my new school, makin' new friends, gettin' on with life. Second grade was great. The school was small but nice, painted white with a bell that rang like a church callin' folks to Sunday mornin'. Of course, everybody was wantin' to know who the new kid was. That's how small towns are—they don't miss nothin', and they sure don't forget a new face.

My first day at school was excitin' but stressful. Those kids stared at me all day like I was some kinda alien who'd landed on their playground. I just stared back at 'em, holdin' my head high, tryin' not to let my knees knock. Eventually, they got tired of lookin', and I'd flash a smile, laugh a little, and let 'em know I wasn't scared. Not really. Maybe a little. But you don't let 'em see that.

As the day went on, I was settlin' into the classroom, watchin' the chalk dust rise like smoke when the teacher wrote our lessons. Seemed like every kid in there already knew each other and shared stories and secrets I wasn't part of yet. I'd only met that one boy on the walk to school, but in time, I figured I'd get to know the rest. Heck, they had to get to know me—they'd stared at me enough that my face was probably etched into their brains like a photograph. Whether they liked it or not, I was part of their world now.

It was gettin' close to lunchtime, and boy, I was hungry. That kind of hunger that creeps up your spine and makes your jaw ache. As we filed into the lunchroom, the clatter of trays and voices bounced off the walls. We all got in line, the scent of canned green beans and fried mystery meat hangin' in the air like a fog. Most kids had to pay for lunch, but my grandma told me I got free lunch. Said it real plain, like she was tellin' me how to tie my shoes—just a fact of life.

I was goin' through the line, wide-eyed and stackin' up my tray like it was a Sunday buffet. I piled on whatever I could—two helpings of mashed potatoes, a slice of meatloaf, some kind of fruit cocktail that looked like it had been swimmin' in syrup for a decade. And then the desserts—three of 'em—puddin' cups and a brownie that looked near-about homemade. I thought, man, I like this—I can come to school and eat all I want.

As I approached the lady at the cash register, she gave me the funniest look, like I was either brave or stupid. Maybe both. She started ringin' up the food, clickin' her little buttons, her lips pursed like she'd swallowed a lemon. I remember the price to this day—three dollars and thirty-five cents. In today's world, it'd probably run you a solid twenty-five bucks. I was standin' there, tray full and heart sinkin'. We just sorta stared at each other like we was in a duel, and she was waitin' for me to dig into my pocket and pull out a handful of bills.

"I get free lunch," I told her, plain and hopeful. She laughed, not mean, but surprised. Then she asked my name. "Larry Bowen," I said. She pulled out this wrinkled sheet, eyes runnin' down the list like she was readin' the Bible. And boom—there it was.

"Yes, your name is on the list for free lunch," she said. What a wave of relief. I thought, *whew, now I can* go eat.

Not so fast, young man.

"You gotta put all that back," she said, pointin' to my overloaded tray like it was a crime scene.

I thought my world had ended. The kids behind me started laughin', gigglin' and elbowin' each other. That laughter cut through me like a rusty knife. The lady told me what I could have for free lunch: one entrée, two vegetables, and a carton of milk. I went from feastin' like a king to what felt like scraps on a prison tray. But the truth was, that was just the way it worked. Most of them kids didn't even know what free lunch meant—just that only the poor kids got it.

I finished my lunch, quiet and low in my seat. Learned a big ol' lesson in humbleness that day. Never made that mistake again. Lesson learned.

As school let out that afternoon, I was ready to go home. It was winter, the kind that nips at your ears and turns your breath into smoke. The sun was slippin' behind the hills early, and I knew I had chores waitin' on me. That dirt basement with coal and wood was callin' my name, but I wasn't in no hurry to answer.

As I walked up the front steps to the porch, I could smell my grandma's cookin' from halfway down the road. That smell was better than any alarm clock, I tell you. Biscuits in the oven, fried chicken poppin' in the skillet, and potatoes that made your mouth water. I was starvin'.

"Wash your hands and get to the table," she hollered, apron tied tight and her hands still dusted in flour. "We got chores to do." Grandma didn't play. She was a worker bee, through and through.

As I sat down, she looked over at me. "How was school today?"

I hesitated. Picked at my potatoes for a second. But then I told her what happened with the lunch lady. Told her about the food and the embarrassment. She laughed—soft, not mean. The kind of laugh that understood.

"Did it embarrass you?" she asked, eyes kind and steady.

"Yes, Grandma. I didn't know what to do, but the lady helped me. The kids laughed at me about gettin' free lunch."

She had a way with words, my grandma. She looked me right in the eyes and said, "My son, don't let that bother you. One day, you'll probably be able to buy everyone's lunch."

Somehow, that settled something in me. I smiled. "Yes, Grandma. One day."

After supper—biscuits so fluffy they melted on your tongue, fried chicken that crunched like heaven, and enough potatoes to stick to your ribs—I was stuffed. But the night wasn't done.

"Time to get to the basement," Grandma said, already stackin' plates in the sink. "Coal and wood don't bring itself up."

So I took off to the basement. I had three five-gallon buckets to fill with coal and my little hatchet to chop the Kindling. Those old wooden steps creaked under my feet like they were warnin' me not to come down. I felt around in the dark for the hanging bulb, heart thumpin'. Finally found the cord and gave it a yank. That dingy lightbulb lit up—barely. Wouldn't light up a shoebox.

But it did light up a mouse—eyes glowin' like tiny headlights. I dropped everything and ran up those steps hollerin'. "There's a rat down here, Grandma!"

She came to the top of the stairs, arms crossed. "He won't bother you. Go on back down."

I went. Shakin' like a tree in a hurricane. He was gone, but not forgotten. I knew he'd be back.

I filled the buckets, one heavy scoop at a time. Those coal chunks were big as softballs. Then I found the hatchet, chopped up a small armload of wood, and got ready to haul it upstairs. The wood wasn't too bad. But them coal buckets—Lord have mercy. One of 'em weighed more than I did.

"I can't do it, Grandma," I called up.

She didn't miss a beat. "No such word as *can't*, son. Hurry up, it's gettin' late. That rat might come back."

Boy, that lit a fire under me. I worked like a dog draggin' those buckets, one by one, up those creaky steps and onto the porch. I got 'em behind the stove just as the night took hold.

I felt proud. Tired and sore, but proud. I'd done it. Knew I'd have to do it again tomorrow, and the day after that. But that was life. No coal, no wood, meant no heat. What don't kill you makes you stronger.

And that basement rat? He might've run off, but I reckon he was watchin'. Just like Grandma. Just like life.

# CHAPTER 16
# GROWING UP FAST
# BECAUSE I HAVE TO

So you're thinkin'—why does *an* 8-year-old boy have to grow *up* so fast? That's a fair question, and if you'd asked me back then, I probably would've looked at you with tired eyes and coal-smudged hands and said, *"Because I got no choice."* Heck, I was already workin' like a grown man, haulin' coal into the house the night before, my little arms trembling under the weight. I'd gone to bed with soot under my fingernails and dreams of just maybe sleepin' in the next morning. But dreams don't last too long when you livin' with a woman like my grandma.

I woke up at 6 a.m., the cold already reachin' under the covers, nippin' at my toes. My bed was one of them big ol' feather ticks, deep and soft like sleepin' in a biscuit. And Lord, I did not want to leave it. The kind of warm that hugs you back. But the world don't stop 'cause you're comfortable.

I crawled out, feet hittin' that icy floor, and I shuffled over to the frosted window, breathin' a little circle into the glass so I could see outside. Everything—*everything*—was white. Snow had come in the night, silent and soft, coverin' the world like a clean slate. I stood there for a second, just starin', and all I could think about was that long walk through the woods to school. My heart sank a little. That snow meant cold boots, wet socks, and breathin' air that hurt your chest.

But while I was starin' out that window, somethin' else found its way to me—the smell of biscuits and sausage gravy. It floated up from the kitchen like a blessing, thick and savory, with that peppery bite that hits your nose first. Boy, did it smell good? I swear, I can still smell it today in my dreams—like it got stitched into my memory along with every other part of my childhood.

Grandma was already up, of course, hummin' and movin' around in her housedress and slippers, rollin' out dough with arms that could've wrung the water from a stone. The clatter of the cast iron, the hiss of sausage in the skillet, the soft thud of dough hittin' the floured counter—all of it made the kitchen feel alive. She didn't sleep much. She worked. That was her way.

I thought all I had to do this morning was eat my breakfast and head on to school.

But then I saw that look—you know, the one. Every Southern grandma's got it. That look that means, *"You got somethin' to do before you even think about leavin' this house."*

And boy, was I right.

Grandma put down her spoon, turned to me with that no-nonsense voice and said, "Take the bucket of coal shakings from the stove and go spread it on the garden."

I blinked. "But Grandma, there's snow all over the garden."

She didn't even pause. "All the better," she said, wipin' her hands on her apron. "When the snow melts, it'll carry that coal dust down into the soil. Makes the ground strong for next spring."

Spring? I wasn't thinkin' 'bout no spring. I was thinkin' about freezin' my little behind off out there in the cold, gettin' black dust all over me before I even got to school. But if Grandma told you to do something, you did it. No room for arguin'. No room for feelin' sorry for yourself.

So I grabbed the dented bucket of coal dust and headed out the back porch, the screen door slammin' behind me with that familiar creak and pop. For a second, I was grateful—there wasn't a whisper of wind. Just that deep, powdery quiet that only comes after fresh snow. The whole world felt still like it was holdin' its breath.

I trudged out to the garden, my boots crunchin' through the snow, and just as I went to shake the dust out over the rows—*whoosh!* A gust of wind hit me dead in the face like it had been hidin' behind a cloud just waitin' for me. The coal dust exploded back on me like a black fog.

I froze. I mean, it froze *solid.* I could feel that fine black grit stickin' to my cheeks, my ears, even up my nose. I looked down at myself—I looked like Buckwheat caught in a chimney sweep. I couldn't believe it.

"I *can't* go to school lookin' like this!" I hollered as I stomped back toward the house, tears springin' up before I even made it to the porch.

And there she was. Grandma. Standin' on the back steps with her hands on her hips, just laughin' so hard she had to lean on the doorframe. Not mean, just that deep, belly laughter of somebody who's seen worse and knows you'll survive.

I was not laughin'. I was cryin', snifflin', spittin' out coal dust.

She came down with a wet washcloth and started wipin' me clean like I was a pig at the county fair. That rag was warm and rough and smelled like Ivory soap. She got me from head to toe—my neck, my ears, even behind 'em.

When she finished, she looked me over and said, "Well, I don't see no blood. I think you'll survive."

I managed a small laugh, still poutin' a little, but I was startin' to see the humor in it. I wasn't happy about it, not yet, but it was over.

"Time to get to school," she said, tappin' me on the back. "This too will pass."

And Lord, was I glad to get out of that cold, wet garden.

As I stepped into the living room, I was hit by a wave of warmth that made my cheeks sting. The coal stove in the corner was workin' overtime, throwin' out heat like a furnace in a dragon's belly. The windows were fogged with sweat, beads of water rollin' down like the house itself was breathin' heavy.

Grandma never heated the bedrooms—said it was a waste. Only the kitchen and living room got the heat. But she made sure those two rooms stayed warm enough to roast a pig. Felt like it was 100 degrees in there. Not really, but you get the idea. That heat wrapped around me like a quilt, and for a moment, I just stood there soakin' it up.

Once I'd thawed out a bit, I took off to meet my friend for the walk to school, headin' through the snowy woods we knew like the backs of our hands. And let me tell you—those woods were somethin' else that morning. The creek was lined with ice, and the water ran underneath like a glass river, tricklin' soft and cold. Snow lay thick on the branches, and the logs across the creek were glazed in frost like nature had frosted a cake just for us.

It looked like a painting. One of them pictures you'd see in a store window at Christmas time, with glitter glued on the snow.

And then—it happened. The most beautiful thing I have ever seen.

A red cardinal—bright as fire and calm as Sunday morning—landed right beside me on an icy log. He tilted his little head, lookin' at me with those black bead eyes, and he didn't fly off. Not right away. He just looked at me like he had somethin' to say.

And I swear to this day, that little bird told me, *You're gonna be alright.*

The snow started flurryin' again, soft and quiet like the sky was whisperin'. That cardinal bent down, took a tiny drink from the icy water, then chirped once—clear and sharp—and flew off into the trees.

As I watched him go, I felt somethin' settle inside me. My day hadn't been so bad after all. That little bird—he helped me see things differently. All he wanted was a drink of water, and he was happy.

I finally made it to school that morning. The snow stopped. The sun peeked through the clouds, throwin' gold on all that white, and it felt like the whole world was smilin' down on me.

It was like the world was sayin', *You're growin'* up, little boy. *Pay* attention. *Nature's tryin'* to teach you *somethin'. Slow down. Breathe deep. And don't forget to* stop and smell the roses.

Even when they're covered in snow.

# JUST A SMALL TOWN SOUTHERN BOY

# CHAPTER 17
# GRANDMA BELIEVES IN WORK

The school day was over, and so it was time to head home to get my chores done. The snow and ice were slowly meltin'—the kind that makes the ground slushy and your socks soggy if your boots got even the tiniest hole in 'em. The streets were thawin' out, gettin' wet with little rivers of meltwater rollin' toward the gutters. But the sky was clearin' up, startin' to show that soft, blue winter sky that somehow feels closer than in summer. That kind of sky feels like it's keepin' an eye on you.

I met up with my friend for the walk home. Mark he was a good kid, steady and quiet, with a walk like he had nowhere to be and all day to get there. Everything was great as we followed our usual path, laughin' and talkin' about nothin' and everything at the same time. When we got near my grandma's house, I told Mark I'd see him tomorrow.

But as I came up to the house, I saw a car parked out front.

Now, let me tell you somethin'—every time I saw a car at a house I lived in, it never meant anything good. It always stirred somethin' in my belly, like a knot tightenin' up with every step closer. Cars meant news, and news in my world usually wasn't the kind you wanted to hear.

I pushed open the front door, and there was a man sittin' at the kitchen table talkin' to my grandmother. She was standin' by the stove with her arms crossed, listenin' close, her face thoughtful but kind. When I stepped in, she turned to me and said, "Come here, I want you to meet someone."

The man stood up, reached out his hand, and said, "I'm a route manager for the local newspaper. We're lookin' for a paperboy to take over a route—the last boy quit."

My grandma, Lord love her, was already sellin' me like I was prize stock at the county fair.

She said, "This here's my grandson. He's a hard worker."

I looked up at her, eyes wide. "Why me?" I asked, bewildered. "I'm only eight years old!"

The route manager chuckled and said my grandma had spoken real highly of me. He leaned forward like he was lettin' me in on a secret but then added, "There's a small problem."

*Small problem,* I thought—now *we're* talkin'. Maybe I'd get out of this yet. I didn't know a thing about paper routes except that it sounded like a whole lotta walkin'. I sat real still, holdin' my breath.

He explained that I had to be twelve years old and have a cosigner to carry papers. I about jumped outta my chair with relief.

"Whew," I whispered to myself. "I'm good."

But if you knew my grandma, you'd know she wasn't gonna let a little ol' detail like *rules* get in the way of what she thought needed doin'. She was determined—and when she set her mind to somethin', Lord help whoever got in her way.

She worked it out. Before I knew it, the route manager and my grandma both signed the paperwork right there at the kitchen table. He was gonna cosign with her.

Then he asked her, "Mind if I take the boy out and show him the paper drop? Go over the route with him?"

So here we go—me sittin' stiff in a stranger's car, ridin' through parts of town I'd never seen, up hills that made my stomach turn and down hills that made me think of that rusty ol' roller coaster at the state fair.

I sat there, lookin' out the window, thinkin' I could never do this, not with all that walkin', and not carryin' some heavy bag stuffed with papers.

But the manager, he kept talkin' like he was sellin' me a dream. "It's not that bad," he said. "You'll like it."

"When do I start?" I asked, my voice thin.

"Tomorrow morning," he said, as easy as you please. "Your paper drops at 5:30 a.m."

I about threw up in my lap.

He handed me a thick book with names, addresses, and little scribbled notes beside them. Special instructions for certain houses— "don't knock," "tuck behind the screen door," "avoid a dog." I wasn't just gettin' papers to people—I was bein' drafted into a secret mission.

He gave me two big canvas paper bags a box of rubber bands, and explained the collections schedule—sixty-morning papers and sixty-eight in the evening. Thursday night, Friday night and Saturday morning were for collections, and the bill had to be paid at the Journal building by noon sharp.

That was a five-mile walk downtown. I didn't even *know* what five miles really was, but I knew it sounded far.

I had no idea what I was gettin' into. But one thing I *did* know—I didn't want to disappoint my grandma. She set this up. This was her way of showin' me she believed in me. And that meant everything.

I had to be in bed by 9 p.m. if I had any hope of wakin' up by 4:45 a.m. My little alarm clock was sittin' on the nightstand tickin' away, soundin' like a hammer to my nerves. It was cold—real cold. About 25 to 30 degrees at that time of morning. Ice still hung to the eaves of the porch, and the ground crunched when you stepped on it.

As I was gettin' ready for bed, Grandma stepped into my room, her voice soft but firm.

"Dress warm in the morning," she said.

"Grandma," I mumbled, pullin' the quilt up to my chin, "why do I have to carry papers?"

She didn't pause. "It'll build character in you. Make you strong. One day, you'll understand."

I didn't understand. Not yet. But I nodded. I didn't argue.

I set my alarm, then dived into that feather tick mattress, lettin' it swallow me whole. I was out in minutes.

Felt like five seconds passed before that alarm clock screamed at me. 4:45 *a.m.* I couldn't believe it. My hands fumbled for the lamp switch like I was searchin' for a lifeline. The room was black as pitch and cold. I put on every layer I could find—two pairs of socks, thick pants, a coat two sizes too big. Then I stepped out the front door into a world that felt like it had forgotten the sun.

It was silent. Not a single sound. Just me and the cold.

I'll admit it—I was scared. That dark weighted it, like it pressed against your chest.

Halfway down the road, just as I was startin' to adjust to the quiet, a stray dog jumped out from the trees. My heart nearly jumped outta my mouth—I was ready to run.

But he stopped. Shiverin', tail waggin', his breath showin' in little clouds. He was just a little thing. Looked up at me like he was askin', *You okay, boy?*

"What are you doin' out here in the cold?" I whispered, kneelin' down. "Where's your home?"

He didn't answer, of course. Just gave me that look and started walkin' with me, his tail waggin' with each step. We climbed that hill together like two soldiers goin' off to war.

We got to the paper drop house, and I was hopin' those papers were already sittin' there. But nope. Not yet. So me and my new friend just sat there on the cold sidewalk, waitin'. He curled up by my feet, his little body tremblin'.

And then—headlights. Bright and blinding. A big white truck pulled up with a screech. Door opened. The driver flung out three

66

heavy bundles of papers like he was deliverin' bricks and drove off without sayin' a word. Not even a wave.

I stared at those bundles. Thick copper wire held 'em tight. I had no idea how to open 'em. I just sat there, tired, cold, and confused. I turned to my little dog and said, "Now what?"

And he—Lord, I swear it happened—he pawed at the middle of the bundle like he was showin' me what to do.

He was right. You pull the center papers out, and the rest collapse. That little mutt saved me that morning.

Lesson learned: animals are sometimes smarter than we are.

I counted out my papers—sixty-seven. Two extras. Good to know.

I tried to lift that bag, and *oof*—heavy. Not coal-bucket heavy, but close. I slung the strap over my shoulder and gritted my teeth.

"We got work to do," I told the dog. And we did.

That first morning was rough. I had to memorize my route, hit porches just right so I didn't wake nobody up, and make sure every paper landed safe and dry. I was careful. I wanted to do it right.

Took me about an hour and a half, and every step made the bag lighter. By the time I had just one paper left, I felt ten feet tall.

That last house had special instructions—behind the storm door. I didn't know why, but I did what the book said.

As I reached for the door, the inside door opened—and there stood a man, hunched over, with somethin' big on his back. It scared the life outta me.

But he just smiled, soft and kind, and said, "Thank you for puttin' the paper behind the door."

"You're welcome," I whispered. "I'll do it for you all the time."

He had a little dog too, starin' at me like *you're* not the *usual guy.*

He must've seen the confusion on my face 'cause he said, "I was born this way. I'm hunched back."

I didn't know what that meant. Never seen nothin' like it. But I smiled and nodded like I did.

Then he reached into his pocket. I flinched, not sure what he was doin'.

But he handed me a dime.

"A tip," he said. "For takin' care of me. I'll give you one every week."

My eyes got as big as saucers. A dime was a treasure. A reward. And I'd earned it.

I never forgot that dime. Not ever.

When I got home, my little dog followed me up the porch and lay down, tail still.

I bent down and said, "Stay right there. I'll be back soon."

I figured he'd be gone by the time I came out again. But part of me hoped he wouldn't.

Inside, Grandma was up, breakfast ready, the house warm and smellin' like heaven.

"How'd it go?" she asked.

I didn't have time to tell it all, but I smiled and said, "It went okay."

Then I told her about the dime.

She grinned. "What you gonna do with it?"

"It's just a dime," I said. "I ain't gonna buy a bike with it."

She chuckled and said, "Those dimes add up. Start you a piggy bank. You never know—you might get more tips."

# CHAPTER 18
# A FAITHFUL FRIEND

It was now after 7 am, and I had to hustle to eat breakfast and head to school. School started at 8:30 am, and I still had to walk a little over a mile to school. I was already tired from the route I had walked that morning, my legs heavy with the weight of each step. The air was cold, colder than usual for this time of year. I could see my breath misting in front of me as I stood in the kitchen, staring out the window for a moment, trying to summon the energy to get through the day.

So, I hurried to put on my fresh shirt, the fabric stiff and cool against my skin. It didn't feel as comfortable as it should, but there wasn't time to care. I needed to eat something before I headed out, so I gulped down my breakfast—just a few bites of toast and a quick swig of milk, nothing special, but enough to fill the hole in my stomach. My thoughts were already focused on the walk ahead and getting to school on time.

I rushed out the door, trying to make it quick. The screen door slammed behind me with a familiar, rusty squeal. As I stepped down off the porch, something caught my ear—a bark. At first, I thought it was a stray dog passing by, but when I turned, there he was. My new friend was sitting on the porch, his tail wagging furiously like a little metronome, just waiting for me. I hadn't expected him to be there, and the sight of him caught me off guard, making me stop in my tracks.

For a moment, I just stood there, surprised by the happiness in his eyes. He wasn't making a ruckus like other dogs would, but I could tell he was excited to see me. I thought to myself, Well, now I've got a real friend. His eyes were shining with an energy that made me feel like he was waiting for this moment for me to show up. The joy in his expression felt like the sun breaking through a cloud. A true friend, I thought again, my chest swelling with a feeling I hadn't had in a long time.

I turned to him and, with a small chuckle, said, "I gotta get to school, little fella. You stay here. I'll be home after school to go carry the evening papers."

He tilted his head as if he understood me like he was saying, Okay, I'll wait right here for you. But just as I started to walk down the steps, I heard him follow me. At first, I thought I could just keep going, but I couldn't leave him behind. There was something about that little dog that tugged at my heart. "Come on, Buddy," I said, and we started walking together.

The air was cold and damp, the kind of cold that sinks deep into your bones. My feet were already feeling the burn of the walk, and I could feel the weight of the day pressing on me. I kept thinking about what would happen to my new friend while I was at school. Would he be okay? What if he didn't wait for me? Would he find somewhere else to go? The worry gnawed at my stomach, and I tried to push it away, telling myself he'd be fine.

He barked and wagged his tail as he trotted along beside me, and I swear he looked up at me with such confidence as if to say, Don't worry, I'll be here when you get back. His little barks helped soothe me a little, but I couldn't shake the feeling that something might go wrong.

As I arrived at school, I saw him sitting right at my feet, waiting. It felt like the most natural thing in the world. As I stepped inside the school building, I looked back at him and said, "You stay here. I'll be back soon."

He barked, his tail wagging like crazy, and I walked away, hoping that when the bell rang, he would still be there, waiting for me. All day long, though, my mind kept drifting back to him. I couldn't focus on anything else. Would he be there when I got out at 2:30 pm? What if he wandered off? What if he got hurt or lost?

The day seemed to drag on forever. Every minute felt like an hour. I kept glancing at the clock, waiting for it to strike 2:30 finally. The thought of getting to the paper drop and getting my route done before it got dark kept me on edge. The sun started to dip lower in the sky, and I could see the clouds rolling in, thick and gray. It was going to rain soon, and I didn't want to deal with that on my first day of the paper route.

When the bell finally rang, I shot out of the building and ran, my heart pounding in my chest, hoping to see my buddy waiting for me. But when I turned the corner, he wasn't there. My stomach sank. I kept walking, my steps feeling heavier with each passing second. Had someone picked him up? Did he get lost? The questions kept piling up in my mind, and I felt a sense of loss before I even knew for sure what had happened. The emptiness grew inside me, crushing down like a weight I couldn't shake off.

I reached the house where my paper bundles were waiting, and I could feel the drizzle starting to come down. The rain was coming, and I didn't want the papers to get soaked. A wet paper was a ruined paper, and I couldn't let that happen on my first day.

There were three big bundles stacked neatly at the drop, just like they were supposed to be. Two were side by side, with a little gap between them, and the third one was stacked right on top of the others, forming a small pyramid. I bent down to grab the top bundle and was ready to start putting papers in my bag when, to my shock, I found him. My buddy—Rock—was under the third bundle, curled up and hidden, like he had been waiting for me the whole time. He gave a bark, a little tail wag, and I could feel the weight lift off my shoulders in an instant.

I laughed, wiping my eyes with the back of my hand. "Where have you been, little fellow?" I asked. And just like that, he licked my face, like he was telling me it was all going to be okay. I was so happy; my heart felt like it was going to burst. He had been there all along, waiting for me.

"Let's go," I said, my voice thick with emotion. "We've got work to do."

From then on, Rock stayed with me for the entire paper route. He walked right beside me the whole way, never once leaving my side. His loyalty was unlike anything I had ever experienced. A little dog, and yet his devotion was a reminder of the kind of loyalty I had always wished for. My grandma she was my rock, my foundation. And Rock, this little dog, was the same for me. That's when I knew—his name had to be Rock. It just felt right. He was my rock, steady and true, just like Grandma had always been for me.

It rained steadily the whole way through the route, but we made it through together. We didn't take any shortcuts. Every house got its paper, and when we finished, I felt both happy and exhausted. So was Rock. I could tell he was tired, too. He was soaking wet, just like I was, but he stayed with me until the very end.

We headed home, both of us looking forward to the warmth of Grandma's house. I could already smell the fried chicken wafting in the air as we ran up the steps to escape the rain. Grandma was standing at the screen door, looking out at us. She saw Rock, then looked back at me. "Who's your new friend?" she asked, her voice soft but full of curiosity.

I wasn't sure how she'd react. I had hoped she'd understand, but I didn't know. "Rock," I said. It felt like the right name for him, even though we'd only just met.

Grandma looked at him for a moment, then out into the yard, thinking it over. Then, out of nowhere, she said, "Are you hungry, Larry Wayne? Dinner's on the table. Come on and bring your friend in. He's probably hungry, too."

I was stunned. I looked down at Rock, and his tail wagged so fast I thought it might fall off. "You heard her," I said to him. "Let's go eat." Rock looked up at me, his eyes wide with joy, and followed me inside.

Grandma made a plate for him, cutting up the chicken into small pieces and putting it on a paper plate on the floor. Rock dug in, his tail spinning like a little propeller. He was so happy, and I couldn't help but smile. I think Grandma was happy to see him, too.

After we ate, Grandma said, "Larry Wayne, we need to find out who he belongs to."

My heart sank. I didn't want to lose him. But Grandma continued, "We'll give it some time. If no one claims him, he's ours."

After we finished dinner, I turned to Rock and said, "I have to go do my chores." The words felt strange in my mouth, even though they were just a part of my routine. It was time to go to the basement to get the coal in before dark. It wasn't a glamorous task, but it was one of those things that had to be done. I had to carry the heavy buckets of coal up the steep steps and into the living room to keep the fire going. It wasn't a big deal, but I wasn't looking forward to it, especially with the day I'd had.

I wanted Rock to stay with Grandma, though. I really didn't want him in that dark, dank basement. The basement was no place for a dog, especially one as sweet and full of life as him. But I didn't have to say it twice. Rock wasn't standing for that. As soon as I headed toward the back door, he was right there beside me, his paws quick on the wooden floor, following me like a shadow. He wasn't about to let me go down there alone. It was almost like he understood what was going on like he knew the basement wasn't the kind of place he wanted to be either.

I reached the cellar door and started down the narrow, creaky steps, the cold air from the basement wrapping around me, making the hairs on the back of my neck stand up. As I reached the bottom, I glanced up, and there was Rock—he had stopped at the top of the stairs, looking down at me with those big, dark eyes of his. It was like he was saying, No way am I going down there.

I couldn't blame him. The basement wasn't a place I wanted to linger in, either. It was damp, musty, and smelled of mildew like everything had been forgotten down there. The only light came from a weak bulb that flickered when you turned it on, casting long, eerie shadows across the cold stone walls. The floor was uneven, covered in dirt and old bits of wood and coal. But it had to be done, and Rock wasn't about to join me in that dank place. He was smarter than I was at that moment.

He waited at the top of the stairs, standing tall like he was the guard at the gate, ready to make sure nothing bad happened. His ears were perked, eyes focused on me like, Hurry up, let's get this over with. This place is for dogs, not humans.

I couldn't help but laugh. "Like you're not a dog," I muttered. It was as if Rock was almost human. He had a way of making everything feel different like there was a silent understanding between us. He wasn't just a dog; he was a companion.

I started filling up the coal buckets, the weight of them almost too much for my small frame, but I managed. As I carried each bucket up the stairs, I could feel Rock's eyes on me, like he was counting the seconds. He was probably thinking, Come on, let's get out of here. This place isn't fit for anyone, not even you.

I finally made it to the top, where Rock was waiting for me, tail wagging like he was cheering me on. We made our way to the living room, where the coal stove stood, a warm beacon in the corner. I set the buckets down behind the stove and filled it up with fresh coal, the warmth starting to fill the room, pushing back the chill of the damp day. Rock curled up next to the stove, his little body warming up in seconds. Within two minutes, he was out like a light, his breathing steady and slow as he napped, his little belly rising and falling with each breath.

The room was cozy, the fire crackling in the stove. But as much as I wanted to relax, too, it was getting late. I had homework to do, and

Grandma's rules were clear. Bedtime was strict in that house. I had to be in bed by 8:00 pm, no exceptions. She knew I had to get up at 5:00 am the next day to make it to the paper drop on time and get my route finished before school started. I wasn't happy about it, but I knew I couldn't argue. It was a routine, one I had gotten used to.

Still, my mind kept wandering back to Rock. What would Grandma do with him once I went to bed? Was she going to put him outside in the cold? I couldn't bear the thought. He had been through enough, and I didn't want him out there in the dark, in the wet chill of the night.

I finally decided I had to know, so I asked her directly. "Grandma, what's gonna happen to Rock? Is he going outside tonight?"

She looked at me for a long moment, like she was thinking it over. Then, she shook her head, her voice firm as she said, "No way I'm putting that puppy out in the cold. He's been through enough."

A wave of relief washed over me, and I couldn't hold it in. My chest tightened, and I almost started to cry. The thought of Rock being sent outside had been eating at me, and to hear that he was going to stay inside—where it was warm and safe—made everything feel right.

It seemed like Rock knew the deal, too. As Grandma spoke, he got up from his cozy spot by the stove and followed her to the living room, his little paws padding softly across the floor. He didn't want to be anywhere else but by us. He had found his place in the world, and it was right there with us.

I went to bed soon after, my mind finally at ease. The day had been long, and I was exhausted from everything that had happened. I lay down under the covers, my body feeling heavy with the weight of the day's work, but my heart was light. It wasn't just physical tiredness; it was the kind of tiredness that comes from knowing you're exactly where you need to be.

Rock, my little companion, had found his way into my life, and in a way, I had found mine too. That night, I drifted off to sleep quickly. It wasn't just from exhaustion. It was because, for once, I didn't feel alone anymore. Rock was there, safe and warm, beside Grandma, and that made all the difference. It had been a long day, but it felt like the beginning of something good.

And for the first time in a long time, I knew things were going to be okay.

# Chapter 19
# Life Goes On - More Work

As my clock went off, I felt like, wow, I just closed my eyes. Sure enough, it was 5 am—time to roll out. The early morning light barely broke through the curtains, and the sound of the clock seemed so much louder than usual. It felt like I had just fallen asleep, and now, I had to face another day. I wondered where Rock was. It was quiet in the house; nothing was heard except for the gentle clink of coal falling into the warm morning heater. That was strange. Of course, it was dead winter, and the air outside was cold enough to freeze your breath. But the warmth inside the house caught me off guard.

I guessed Grandma got up during the night and put some coal on the stove so the house wouldn't be cold when I woke up. The house was toasty warm, which was unusual. Usually, the house was cold in the morning because the coal stove burned out during the night. But not this morning. It made me wonder what was going on. Grandma had a way of doing things that made everything feel just a little more magical, especially on mornings like this.

As I got my clothes on and grabbed my paper bag to get out the door to deliver my papers, I headed toward the living room. The warm glow of the stove reached me before I even stepped into the room. As I approached the living room, I could feel the heat from ten feet away, like it was wrapping around me, easing the chill from the morning air. But to my surprise, I figured out why we had heat this morning. There lay Rock, fast asleep by the stove, all warm and cozy.

I smiled as I watched him, his little body curled up tight, his breathing steady and soft. He didn't move an inch. He was snoring lightly, so peaceful. Now I knew why Grandma warmed up the stove so early—it was for Rock, not me! *Lol,* she really liked that dog. That made my morning. That little dog had a way of bringing warmth into the house, not just from the stove but from the joy he brought to everything.

I chuckled softly, watching him. He didn't have a care in the world, just curled up, warm and comfortable, while I had to get out there in the cold. I wasn't jealous, though. It made me feel good to know that Rock was being cared for just as much as I was.

I was heading to the front door to slip out without waking up Grandma or Rock. They could just sleep in. I'd be back in an hour or so. It was a cold morning, but no snow or sleet—just the kind of chilly air that made the world feel still, waiting for the sun to rise. The sun had not started to show its face yet. I thought, *Maybe* by the time I get to my drop, the sun will make an appearance. I loved the sunrise. Everything felt fresh and new like the world was waking up for the first time that day.

As I turned the door lock to sneak out, it clicked louder than I thought it would. *Click.* The sound seemed to echo through the quiet house. And as I started to open the old, creaky door, I heard a Woof*!* There was Rock, standing in the doorway like, *You're* not leaving without me, are you*?*

I had told him to stay home this morning, but he whimpered and almost begged to go. His eyes were wide and full of that pleading look. His tail was wagging, making little circles. What do you do in a moment like that?

I bent down and said, "Come on, let's go to work." He was already leading the way out like he knew exactly where we were going. And sure enough, he did. He started up the hill to the drop like a proud dog, his little legs moving quickly. I could hardly keep up with him.

He would stop and wait for me, like *Are* you coming or not*?* His tail wagging so fast it was like it might fly off. "I'm coming, Rock, slow down!"

The morning went by fast. No problems at all. Rock and I finished the route much quicker than I had the day before. As I was learning the route, I was getting better at it, moving faster with each drop. I picked up a new subscriber, which was all the way down the street, next to the main road, on the corner. I had the address but no name.

As I got to the corner, I saw the building. It was a Dunkin' Donuts. Rock and I looked at each other—WOW, donuts*!*

But I had a problem—I had no money. Rock didn't understand that, though. His ears perked up, and he was just as excited as I was. I couldn't help but laugh. As I entered the front door, I told Rock to stay. He couldn't come in there. I knew he wanted to follow me, but I also knew the shop wasn't the right place for him.

A man was putting donuts in the glass covers. He was the only one in the shop at that time. He turned around and asked, "Can I help you?" Of course, I was a little nervous. I wasn't sure if I had the wrong place, but I told him I had the paper for here.

He smiled at me, a nice, happy, chunky man. "Of course, I'm the manager. That's great!" He seemed genuinely excited to be getting his paper.

He looked at me and asked my name. "I'm Larry. What's yours?"

"Henry," he said. "Who's your friend out there?"

"That's Rock, my dog. He's a good friend."

He smiled again. "It's good to have good friends."

"You must be the new paperboy," he said as if he'd figured it out the moment he saw me.

"Of course," I said. "Yes, sir."

He grinned. "You must be a pretty good paperboy. Did you bring my paper in? The other one just threw it at the glass door and left. Rain or snow, he didn't care. Never even said hello. But he didn't last long."

He looked at me and said, "You must be cold and hungry."

I nodded. "Yes, sir. You're my last paper drop-off today. I'm heading home to get ready for school. My dog is waiting on me."

Henry smiled kindly. "Do you have time for a donut and a cup of coffee?"

Of course, I did, but I knew I didn't have any money. Then he just said, "It's on me—and your friend. I'll get him a donut, too."

I was shocked. I didn't dream something like that would happen. Henry and I were becoming friends. He asked me what flavor I wanted. Of course, I had no idea—I had never seen so many donuts in my life. My eyes were wide with excitement, and I could feel Rock's excitement, too, as he waited patiently by the door.

I asked him, "What's your favorite?"

He said, "Honey dipped."

"That sounds good. I'll have that one too."

He got one for Rock, too. Rock was ecstatic. His little tail was wagging so hard it looked like it was going to take off. We sat down and ate and drank some coffee. Man, was that good. For a few moments, I felt like I was in heaven. The warmth of the coffee and the donuts settled into me, making everything feel just a little bit perfect.

As we finished up the donuts, I told Henry I had to go. "I've got to get ready for school."

He asked, "You look awfully young to be carrying papers."

I nodded. "Yes, sir. I'm 8 years old. I live with my grandmother."

He paused, then said, "Wait a minute. I have something for you."

"Okay," I said.

He went behind the double doors and came out with a box full of donuts to take home to my grandmother. I tried to protest, "You don't have to do that." But he insisted.

He wanted to, and he told me he was impressed with me, so young and working. "Larry, if you bring me my paper every morning, I'll give you a donut and coffee every morning—and your friend gets a donut too."

I was amazed that someone could be so nice. I told him, "I'll see you tomorrow morning. I hope."

He smiled. "You stay safe out there—and your friend."

As Rock and I headed home with the box of donuts, I could smell them, and the box was still warm from the donuts. The sweet scent filled the air around us. I knew Grandma would be asking questions about the donuts.

As Rock and I entered the house, it was toasty warm, and we could smell the bacon cooking. Rock went crazy from the smell, his little nose twitching with excitement.

I set the donuts on the kitchen table. Grandma had her back to us, busy at the stove. As she turned around, she asked how the morning went, and then she saw the donuts. She gasped, "Wow, where did you get them, and how?"

I smiled and said, "I have a new customer—it's a Dunkin' Donuts. How cool is that? I met the manager this morning. His name is Henry. He sent these to you and gave Rock and me a donut and coffee this morning, just for bringing the paper inside to him. He was so nice."

Grandma looked pleased. "That's great. See what happens when you do people right? Let's have a donut. Tell Henry to thank you when you see him again."

"Tomorrow, Grandma."

We ate breakfast, and I had to get going. The morning was disappearing fast—school time was creeping up on me.

I was fixing to leave when I looked for Rock. He was passed out at the coal stove, sound asleep. I thought, *Well,* I guess *I'm* going to school by myself today.

Grandma told me, "Go on to school. Rock is tired this morning. He'll be here when you get home this afternoon to carry papers."

"Okay, Grandma. I'm gone. Bye, Rock," I said quietly as I headed out the door. I missed him going to school today, but I knew he was safer at home with Grandma.

The morning was beautiful—crisp air and clear. It was nice. Life was good for now, but I knew in my heart, *Would* it stay this way? I had stability in my life—it was different, something I had never had before.

My first week on the paper route was a new experience. It was time to collect the paper bill from my customers. It started on Thursday evening, Friday evening, and Saturday morning. My first bill was on my Thursday morning paper drop under the bundled wire. I was nervous—I had no idea how much it would be, but I had to look at the balance due, which I didn't even understand but would learn quickly.

I pulled it out of the brown envelope to look at the bill. It was $31.65 for the week. To me, that was a fortune. My stomach twisted as I stared at that amount. I just prayed I could cover it. I didn't even know what I was going to make for the week.

I had till Saturday noon to get the bill paid downtown, and I got a little nervous, but I knew it would be okay. I had Grandma, and she always knew what to do when I got confused. As the week ended and I went collecting from my customers, I had a lot of change to count. Saturday morning, I was home, counting my money to cover my bill. All that money was on my bed as I started to count it—coins scattered everywhere, like a jigsaw puzzle of copper, nickels, dimes, and quarters.

My Grandma came into the bedroom and asked me if I needed some help. I said, "YES!" quickly. She sat with me, and we figured it out together. My heart raced, wondering if it was going to be enough. I worried it wasn't going to be enough.

Grandma told me, "I don't think you have to worry. You'll be fine."

After we finished counting the money, it came to $42.50. My grandma said, "You made a profit—$10.85."

I asked Grandma, "That's all mine?"

"Yes," she said with a smile. "That's what you made."

I thought it was a fortune! But I worked hard for that $10.85. Getting up at 5 in the morning is no picnic. I worked about 17 hours a week—morning and evening, fighting bad weather and cold rain. It wasn't a picnic.

I had to figure out what that came to an hour. My Grandma helped me.

As I sat on my bed trying to figure out my hourly salary, I was a little confused after I counted all the money. My Grandma helped me to figure everything out. After she got the numbers together, she asked, "Are you ready to hear what you made per hour for all your work?"

I was a little excited but didn't really have a concept of hourly rates. I just threw newspapers. Grandma said it came out to 64 cents an hour.

I asked her, "Is that good?"

She smiled and said, "It's better than nothing per hour."

In the 60's, the hourly rate was $1.10 an hour by government standards. I didn't even make minimum wage. *That's* not good, but hey, I'm 8 years old—I felt rich.

Maybe I'll make more next week. I look back on that time now, and it was tough. Little did I know it was building me for later times in life. My grandma asked me what my plans were for my first paycheck. Heck, I didn't know. But I knew what I wanted.

I had always wanted a new pair of Converse tennis shoes—Carolina blue, just like the Tarheels of UNC. I didn't know how much they cost, but these Pic and Pay tennis shoes hurt my feet. These plastic cheapos weren't working out.

I'd seen some other boys wearing those Converse shoes. *They* were the bomb. If you had a pair of those, you were in. My first pair of tennis shoes at Pic and Pay, which my Grandma bought for me, were like $1.75, so I thought, *How* much will those *Converse cost?*

As the week ended on Saturday, I was heading downtown to pay my paper bill. I was a little nervous with this money on me. I walked by myself, but it was good in those days—you didn't have to worry about getting robbed. I just wanted to get this paper bill taken care of. The sooner, the better.

I walked by a sporting goods store downtown on Fourth Street. It was a fancy store—nothing I had ever seen. It looked expensive. I thought, *Man,* who shops there? *Not* me.

As I walked by the picture window, I could see all the sporting goods in the store. MAN, it was a lot of stuff, and I'm sure none of it was cheap. I was glancing in the picture window for anything Carolina blue. I was excited. I hope *they're* open when I start home from paying my paper bill.

As I made my way to the journal to pay my bill, all I had on my mind was a pair of Converse. The Journal was really close by, so I didn't have far to go. As I entered the lobby at the bill payment counter, there was a line. I was the youngest one in there—most of the paper carriers looked like teenagers, which they probably were.

A man at the counter noticed me and asked, "Can I help you?"

And, of course, I said, "Yes. I'm here to pay my bill for my route."

He said to me, "How old are you? Where's your Dad?"

I said, "I don't have one." He looked confused.

"You look awful young," he said.

I said, "Well, I am. I'm 8 years old."

He said, "How did you get a paper route?"

"Mr. Meadows got it for me."

He looked at me like, *How* do you know Mr. Meadows?

He said, "Well, that changes everything. Do you have your bill?"

"Yes, sir. It's right here, and I have the collections to pay it."

He said, "You're pretty smart, little guy."

I laughed and said, "Not really—I just throw papers!"

As we walked up to the counter, he asked for the money. I had all the coins, and they were heavy. I was glad to get rid of them. He took the bag of change and dumped it into a machine to count it. I had never seen one—I didn't really know what it was. All I knew was it was banging crazy, jumbling coins. The total on the screen came to $42.50.

"Your invoice is $31.65. The balance is yours," he said.

I said, "I understand."

The man asked me if I figured it up myself. "Of course not—my grandma helped me."

"It looks like a profit for you. $10.85," he said.

"Yes. I worked hard for that," I said. He nodded, "That's pretty good for an 8-year-old boy."

I laughed because all I had on my mind was Converse.

The man handed me my receipt and my profit, and I told him I would see him next week. As I headed out the door, I was on a mission to get to that sporting goods store.

I was only about 5 minutes away. As I walked toward the sporting goods store, my heart was racing to go in and check things out in that fancy store. A man who worked there came up to me and asked if he could help me.

I said, "Yes, sir."

The next question he asked me—*you know what it was*: *"Where's your daddy?"*

"I don't have a daddy. I live with my grandma," I said.

He said, "Really?" Like he didn't believe me, but he did.

He asked me, "What are you looking for specifically?"

I said, "What does that mean, *'specifically'*?"

I really wanted to see some Converse tennis shoes—Carolina blue, like the Tarheels.

He immediately said, "They're expensive."

I worried then.

"We have a whole section of Carolina Tarheels stuff. Come on, come with me."

I was so excited I almost peed my pants.

As we approached the display, it was all Carolina blue. It was the most beautiful thing I had ever seen. What size shoes do you wear?

I said, "I think I'm in a 6."

So, you want some Tarheel Converse? I'll go in the back and bring out a pair in size 6.

I waited patiently, nervous because he never told me how much they were. I sat down on the bench as he came with the box. "Here you go. Size 6." They were beautiful—I could see them on my feet, heading to school with everyone looking. Chuck Taylor was the bomb at that time. If you had a pair of these boys, you were the big dog.

As I took them and slipped into them, they were so soft, especially after wearing those plastic Pic and Pay things.

The salesman smiled and said, "They look good on you."

They feel wonderful. How much?

I was dying to find out. If I had to leave these shoes, I would never be the same again.

He said, "They're $8.65."

"REALLY?" I hollered. I scared him to death.

I was figuring in my head how much I had left if I bought the Converse. I had a little over $2.00, I was guessing. He said, "Do you have enough?"

I said, "I'm pretty sure I do."

He said, "You need some socks with these shoes. They're 50 cents a pair. They're athletic socks—they'll feel even better when you put these on with the Converse. How about 2 pairs?"

That was another $1.00. My money was leaving fast—all that work I did, and the money was leaving my hand in 5 minutes. I couldn't figure that out.

I was wondering what my grandma would say if I came home almost broke!

After the salesman figured it all up, it was on the backdoor of $10.00. Then he said, "I have to figure the tax." Of course, stupid me said, "What's that?" The salesman laughed.

By the time he finished, I was nearly broke, except for a little change jingling.

I told him, "Let's forget the socks."

But he insisted, "You need the socks with those shoes."

I said, "That will take all the money for the week I carried newspapers."

He said, "So, you're a paperboy?"

"My son is too. I'm impressed. I'll throw in the socks if you buy the Converse."

"REALLY?" I said.

"Yes, it's a deal."

I was the happiest boy in North Carolina at that one moment. He said, "Are you going to wear them home?"

Of course, I didn't want them to ever come off my feet, like the ruby red slippers in *The* Wizard of Oz.

I thanked him for everything. As I left that store, my feet had never felt so proud. I couldn't take my eyes off of them as I started home. I had to get going—I had to throw papers soon.

# CHAPTER 20
# MY WORLD IS GETTING BETTER

Everyday I Think

As I headed home in my new Converse, I held the box they came in with an ear-to-ear grin. I couldn't help it; I was just proud of it. Getting your hands on a Converse wasn't somethin' you could not celebrate. As I made my way in, I wondered what my grandma was going to say when she'd know I blew all my money on a pair of shoes. I walked in the house, strutting my stuff in these shoes.

My grandma was making her way into the living room and saw the pretty Converse I was tryin' to hide. I failed. She saw the new Carolina blue Converse and then looked at me, who was grinning sheepishly.

She chirps, "Well, I see you did it. I see what you're tryin' to do. I done cleaned your drawers, kid — you cain't hide nothin' from your grandma."

She just smiled and said, "They're very nice. Take good care of them."

Guess my grandma was wiser than I thought she was. She knew what the kicks meant for me. They were the nicest thing I had ever had; plus, for a kid who hadn't seen many good days and had been hustling from his wee days, they were very special. My grandma certainly seemed proud of them and me. Seeing my glee and gratitude, she added, "You earned them. See what hard work does for you?"

As she turned around to head back to the kitchen, I took my box into my bedroom and set it up on the dresser like a trophy. I centered it right in the center of the dresser. I was so proud of that box, just about as much as the shoes themselves.

Later in the day, I had to head out to carry my papers for the afternoon. My feet had never felt so good. It was the rapture of owning a Converse that made the whole deal more comforting than the actual shoes. I couldn't wait to get finished for the day. All through the paper route, I would take a pause and admire my feet, my new kicks looking sharp. Those shoes looked like a new trophy, shiny and so clean. I was almost tiptoeing around in them, being careful to keep them clean. I knew they would eventually get dirty, but as long as I could keep them looking fancy... Plus, Grandma was some solace for me, a savior. I knew she could wash them for me if I asked.

The foolish child in me thought everyone was watching me because I had these special shoes. You know, the "all eyes on me" feeling of a kid! Of course, they were not; they couldn't care less. But that didn't matter to me. I was just a proud boy trying to show off, but not really.

I finally got home from my paper route and knew I had more chores lined up to do. The very next one had me freeze in dread. I had to get my coal in for the night. I thought, *OH NO! I can't wear these in that basement.* Understandably, I had to put the "Pick and Pay" shoes on to go to the basement. Well, the cheapos had a purpose, after all. I carefully and meticulously put my Converse on top of the box. They were gleaming in the mirror, not really but can't explain that to a kid. I loved them shoes. I headed out to do my chores so I could eat my dinner and get ready for bed.

As I finished up for the day, Grandma and I had dinner. She looked at me, clearly picking up on the delight I was brewing in, and said, "You like those shoes, don't you?"

"Yes, Grandma, they're the best thing I have ever had in my eight years on earth," I reply, smiling.

"Are you going to wear them to school tomorrow?" She asked me.

"Of course, I am." I couldn't wait to walk into that school with those shoes on my feet. The thought of the glam and bling, my friends rounding up to admire my new kicks, tickled me.

My grandma was all-in with me in all of this. She ordered me, " You gotta get your bath. You cain't be wearin' them shoes when the rest of you's dirt-riddled, boy."

I was ready to get to bed, and I knew 5 am would come early. The evening news was on and some news about the ACC tournament was running on loop. My grandma turned my attention to the TV. "Look who's on the news. It's the Carolina Tarheel basketball team."

The team was being interviewed because the ACC tournament was starting in a week. Grandma chirped, "You see their shoes? They're just like yours."

Man, I felt so good, if I had smiled anymore, all of my 32 teeth would have plopped out. As I left to get my bath and get ready for bed, I glanced one more time in the direction of my shoes to see if they were still on my dresser. They were. For some reason (a child's excitement and love for earning something he loved, of course), I thought they would be gone. Crazy, I guess.

The day had been a good one for me, terrific if you asked an eight-year-old me. I had, through my hard-earned money and hustling door-to-door, bought something that I always wanted. Nobody could have taken those shoes from me; I would have fought the devil himself to keep them.

It was close to 8:30—time to sleep. Again, I looked at the box on the dresser. I checked my shoes one more time to make sure they were centered in the middle of the dresser. It was—my treasure box. I got in the bed, my eyes locked on the box. I didn't know when I fell asleep; I only remembered the details of the logo on the box and that I had wished my shoes night.

"Goodnight, see you in the morning!" I laugh about that still today.

Prayer was a bedtime routine. And now, with my Converse, there was an addendum to my daily nighttime prayers. I thanked God for everything he had done for me, especially my grandma and now my Converse.

No matter how childish and funny it seems now, back then, it was feeling special. Getting something nice was a very special thing for a poor boy. Most kids my age wouldn't have understood what my feeling was like. They didn't have to face life like I did. Their parents would just go out and buy it for them.

The way I see it, those kids are missing out on a rapture unlike anything. Yes, it is nice to have a family and all—Parents who would buy you gifts and remember your birthdays. But for many kids, there are no special moments because they have never known what it is like to do without nice things. I did; getting Converse was very special to me and I cherished them. As I fell asleep, all I could think of was to get those shoes back on my feet tomorrow morning.

5 am struck, and the clock went off. It was time again to carry papers. But when I got up, I heard a prattling at my window. I glanced outside and saw rain slamming down the windowpane and everything else outside. I thought, *I can't wear my Converse in the rain. No way that's happening.* Now, before I am labeled finicky, I would like to remind that these weren't *just shoes.* They were *the shoes.* They were all kinds of special. I realized I would have to wear my "Pick and Pay" shoes out in the rain again.

That was alright for me. This way, I would save my beloved Converse from the disaster of rain. Plus, I had worn "Pick and Pay" forever anyway. I convinced myself that as rain would subside, I could wear them to school today and show them off in their gleaming state to my friends. As I went to go out the front door, the solid door opened easily because it used to swing inward, but the screen door would not budge. I didn't know why. I pushed and pushed, but no hope. I thought, Now what?

Then, all of a sudden, I heard a grunt—like it was a person hurt. I quickly plopped down and peeked from under the screen door. I turned on the porch light and hollered to see if any reply would come. I thought I woke Grandma up. But I was more taken aback by what I saw. There was a lady out there. She was splayed on the porch, apparently beaten up and drunk. I could smell her a country mile away.

She was moaning and when her sloshed eyes rested on me, she said, "Larry Wayne, Larry Wayne, it's your Aunt Margie. Please help me. It so cold that morning."

She would have been an ordinary drunkard to me, but something stuck. I had heard my mom talk of her sister in the past, but I had never seen her before. Mom had told stories about her, but I never thought there was much to it. Plus, I was just a kid; what good I would have been for her anyway.

Still, I tried as best as I could. I gave her directions so she would move aside and the door could open. "Aunt Margie, try to roll over away from the door so I can get out to try to help you."

She nudged herself a little, enough for me to squeeze out of a small gap. My philanthropic eight-year-old self was trying to figure out how I was going to get her in the house to get her warm. Imagine that. I barely knew the lady but still wanted to pull her in saw she was warm. Plus, I was also getting late for my paper route.

I told Aunt Margie, "I am going to try to drag you in, at least to the stove, to get you warm."

She apparently liked the idea. Drunk out of her senses, she was able to register my extended help as she smiled. She was so drunk and beat up that I didn't know what was going to happen next. I wasn't even sure if that was a brilliant idea to let a stranger in but I felt so sorry for her. Grandma, against my better judgment, was still sleeping, which was surprising to me. Rock, too, was uncharacteristically very quiet. He was not barking at the lady, just whimpering like he knew this was not a good idea. Not the brightest mutt, my Rock. I got the door open and started dragging her in. I told Rock to stand and not let the door close on us like he really knew. But he did it. What an amazing dog!

We grunted and pulled Aunt Margie into the room and out of the cold. She was very cold and sore. She lay by the stove, taking in the warmth and almost thawing. I put some more coal in the stove to get the fire blazing. There were only a paltry few embers here and there. The night had consumed most of the coal. After that, I went to get my blanket from my bed to get her as comfortable as I could. I thought that would be sufficient because till I got back from my route, Grandma would be up, and she might take it from there. I had no idea how my grandma was going to react to all this. She might be mad at me for not waking her up.

As I got Aunt Margie the blanket over her, I told her, "I had to go. I would be back in a hour or so."

All drunk Aunt Margie did was smile and pass out again. She was pitiful. I told Rock to stay close to her until I got home from carrying papers. Usually, he was my plus one on my paper route, but dogs have an instinct when things don't seem right, and boy, he knew something was up. He stayed put right down beside her to keep her warmer. The coal stove was heating up well as I had loaded it with the biggest chunks I could find. In fact, it was so hot, the flames were blazing red.

As I headed out into the rain and cold, I worried about my aunt (who I hadn't seen in my life) but she was at least safe for now. "Hopefully, she will be ok," I murmured to myself and went out. I hoped she would come around before I got home.

There were two kinds of thought simultaneously spinning in my head. One— Grandma will probably go crazy when she wakes up and finds the tosspot Aunt Margie in the living room. Two—Grandma would handle it because she had dealt with this before. Mom had told me stories of her sister and that she was an alcoholic and had a troubled life. I didn't want that in my life. One look at her and I thought, *no way I am going down that road.* Most of my relatives drank, but I had never seen anything like my aunt's condition. It was like a horror story.

I got home at about 6:45 am from carrying papers. The rain had quit, but it was still cold. As I came in the front door, I heard a commotion coming from the kitchen. Instantly, I ran towards the slurs flying and the drunken laughter that came out in a jumble. It was terrible what I saw. My grandma had Aunt Margie up in the kitchen, giving her the third degree. When she saw me enter, she sorta smiled, which was her way of saying, "Thank you for letting me in. I can handle Grandma, don't worry."

My grandma, on the other hand, was pissed. "Blowing steam out of her ears" kinda pissed. She gave me a look that said, "I will deal with you later." I dreaded that later. I dashed out because I had to go get ready to get to school and grab a quick bite. As I headed out the door, my Uncle Roy was coming in. I knew then I had to get going. A drunk Aunt—an angry Grandma—Uncle Roy. That was the recipe for trouble. This is not going to be good. As a little boy, I didn't need to be involved in this. My life was so good until that, and my dumbass thought I could fix things by letting my drunk aunt in. I had never really felt secure in my life until I had gone to live with Grandma, and now she had to handle this situation with her daughter. I felt sorry for her, too, but not sorry enough to stay and get a whooping.

# Chapter 21
# Dealing With Family
# Problems And My Life

My grandma dealt with a lot of—well, let's just say it—a lot of CRAP. All her children were always into something: drinking, marital problems, the kind of things that simmered low and slow like a pot of beans forgotten on the back of the stove. After all, she had **fourteen** kids and outlived **five** of them. Just think about that for a minute. Buryin' five of your babies, even if they were grown—no mama ever gets over that. Each one took a piece of her soul with 'em to the grave.

She was getting up in age, her back bowed not just from the weight of the years but from all that sorrow she carried in silence. I felt sorry for her, I truly did. And now she was raising her grandson.

I respected her. She was strong-willed and worked hard her whole life. She'd get up before the rooster crowed, hands in biscuit dough before most folks' feet hit the floor. She didn't take no mess off nobody, but her kind of tough came from love, the kind that don't always hug you but always makes sure you got shoes on your feet and cornbread in your belly.

My Aunt was a mess. Her life got all messed up when her husband killed a man in their house. I was too young to understand all the details, but I remember the tension, how the grown folks whispered in corners like ghosts were listening. After that, she turned to alcohol—the biggest mistake of her life. You could see it in her eyes, the way the light had drained out, replaced by a glassy kind of hurt.

Being around that crap as a kid is hard, but it makes you stronger in life—not to make the same mistakes they made. You learn to see pain coming before it knocks on your door.

About all my uncles drank, except for one of them. I remember their laughter turning to shouting, their Sunday best turning to crumpled shirts and angry hands. Around my grandma's house, it was always quiet—that peaceful kind of quiet where you could hear the wind rustle through the curtains and the ticking of the old wall clock—until one of Grandma's children would come by, which was usually on Sundays.

Grandma always would cook Sunday dinner, and most of her kids would be there every Sunday to eat. The kitchen would fill up with the smell of fried chicken and biscuits and the familiar sounds of clattering pots and gospel radio humming low in the background. In those days, it was pretty much a custom—families would get together to eat and spend time together... and to argue about things, lol.

Grandma was the last key to hold the family together. She was the glue, the old oak tree that everybody leaned on even as they broke her branches.

One thing for sure: I knew what we were having every Sunday— it was fried chicken. Very rarely was it anything different. The basic things. Just a good ole country dinner. You could smell it from afar, that sizzle of grease and the soft clink of the cast iron skillet.

Grandma would always put the chicken legs up for me because I went to Sunday school every Sunday, and I didn't get home until after 12 noon, and the family usually had already eaten. If she didn't put my chicken legs up, they would eat them. The chicken leg was my favorite part of the chicken—still is. Something about that crispy skin, just salty enough, and the way it pulled right off the bone made it feel like a prize just for me.

The family would fill their stomachs up and usually leave right after Sunday dinner. They didn't hang around long—just to eat. I was a kid, and I already had most things figured out. I had never seen them until Sundays to eat. Funny, even though they were my grandma's kids.

The Sunday thing is not prevalent in today's generation. It was a regular thing in the '60s. That generation is gone, and mostly, the families don't do that anymore. But that doesn't mean they shouldn't. The values of things today have dramatically changed. Folks now barely look each other in the eye over dinner, let alone gather together every week. There was something sacred in that rhythm, even if it came with chaos.

When I came in from church, I would just say hi to everyone and head to my room. I usually waited for them to leave, and Grandma would fix my plate, and I would go eat. I wasn't much for all the family problems and listening to all the stuff they talked about, which sometimes just ended up in an argument about nothing that made no sense.

I was happy to see my mom there, but that was about it.

Sundays were a slow day for me. I did get up at 4:30 am to go throw my papers and get home, and head to church. After lunch, I would usually go to my room and take a nap. I didn't have to carry papers on Sunday afternoon, which was like a vacation to me, and I took advantage of it because I knew it would start again Monday morning, 4:30 am sharp, in the cold or rain, with the streets still asleep and only dogs barking at me.

# CHAPTER 22
# DIFFERENT TIME, DIFFERENT
# ERA - RACIAL INEQUALITY

The 1960s were a black-white thing. A whole lot is going on in the world. The KKK, the Black Panthers—a lot of sadness. It was like the whole country was boiling over, and we were caught somewhere in the middle, just trying to live our little lives while the world screamed on the news.

My grandma's house was in an area of town that bordered Black town, or as they called it in that time, Niger Town. That's the word folks used back then, hard and ugly as it sounds now. I hated it even then, though I didn't have the words to say why. It was just how people talked. That part of town was poorer, run-down, but it had a soul to it. Music came through the air on warm nights, and sometimes you'd hear laughter echoing like wind chimes down the alleyways.

Times were getting bad, as rioting and looting were taking place in downtown. We were about a mile from downtown, which I walked to on Saturdays to pay my paper bill. It was a different kind of walk back then, eyes wide open, not just for dogs or bullies, but real danger, the kind that smelled like smoke and fear.

# JUST A SMALL TOWN SOUTHERN BOY

My grandma worried about me being out early morning carrying my papers. One of my routes bordered downtown where the riots were taking place—burning buildings and breaking out windows in retail buildings. I remember the smoke hanging low in the sky like a bruise, the broken glass glinting on the sidewalks like angry stars. The police were everywhere, and they were very vigilant of everything going on.

Then one morning, around 5 a.m., as I was carrying my papers about a block from downtown, a policeman stopped me to talk to me. His cruiser rolled up slow behind me, headlights cutting through the thick morning fog, and I felt my chest tighten like it always did when a grown man looked at me too long.

He asked me, "Son, do you feel safe?" Of course, I said no. My voice was small, but honest.

He was a nice man. Not all of them were. But this one, he looked tired and kind behind his badge. He told me he would meet me at the end of the block every morning to escort me up the street to finish my route and follow me back to get me to safety.

I was really relieved. You can't know how big that felt as a little boy—to have somebody on your side like that, in a time when even walking the streets felt like crossing into enemy territory. I got home that morning and told my grandma not to worry. I had a policeman following me on my route near downtown. That made her feel better—and me too.

We had no idea when the conflicts would end. It was all school segregation, Blacks and the Whites being bussed across town to mix up the schools. I was one who would be bused to Black town to go to school. Of course, I was a kid—I didn't understand a lot of it, as most kids didn't. All I knew was I packed my lunch and rode that bus like I was riding to another world.

As I said earlier, my grandma's house backed up to Black town. My grandma's yard had a barbed wire fence that went along the back border of the property. It looked like something meant to keep wild animals out, or maybe keep us in. I never really paid that much attention to who was behind us. There were blackberries that ran on the fence that I would pick to eat sometimes. Sweet and tart, they'd stain your fingers purple and your soul a little too.

My grandma always told me to never go past that fence—that it was dangerous, which I didn't understand, but I listened to my grandma.

One day, I was at the fence picking blackberries, and I was looking through the fence, and I saw this old Black man in bib overalls plowing his garden. He didn't see me at first. I kept watching him. For some reason, he fascinated me. He seemed like a gentle man. He was very old, and his skin was very leathery—I guess from the weather and the sun over the years.

He was a strong man. He was pushing his plow through the soil, breaking it up into rows to plant. That dirt rolled up behind him like waves. His muscles rippled under his clothes, slow and sure, like he'd done that same motion a million times before.

As I was staring through the blackberries, the man dropped his handkerchief on the ground, and as he was coming up, he spotted me at the fence and smiled. He waved at me.

And I ran back to the house like a rabbit.

I don't know if I was scared or just surprised. My heart was thumping so hard I thought maybe it'd burst out of my chest. I was told to stay away from Black people. He had my curiosity, though. He seemed to me to be a nice man. Of course, I had never been around a colored man—it was forbidden.

I was sitting on the back porch, my knees still dirty from the garden dirt, when my grandma heard the commotion and came out.

"Son, what's the problem?"

Of course, I said, "Nothing."

I was panting and sweating from the run from the back fence.

"Where have you been?"

"At the blackberry vine on the fence. I saw a Black man in his garden, and he saw me and I ran."

My grandma told me to stay away from there and come in the house. She asked me, "Did he say anything to you?"

I said, "No. He just smiled. Grandma, he had the prettiest white teeth I had ever seen—and a nice smile."

My grandma just looked at me and said, "Don't never go past that fence, you hear me?" in a very loud voice. "It's very dangerous."

Which I didn't understand. I'm a 9-year-old kid. "What's dangerous about it, Grandma? He seemed like a nice man."

Grandma said, "Those people are different from us. Stay away."

I was already determined to go back. He had my interest.

Grandma told me, "If I ever see you back there again, I will whip you good."

And Lord, I didn't like those switch whippings. They stung like wasps.

One thing about Grandma's whippings—she had a psychological way of beating you down. When she wanted to correct you for something that deserved the whipping, she would call me to her and give me the butcher knife. Then she'd send me to the bush at the end of the yard to cut the switch I was going to get whipped with.

As a young boy, I would just stand there in front of that bush crying, because I knew if I didn't get a good limb one, I'd get it twice as hard when I got back to my grandma. She would stand on the back porch waiting for me to come back. That slow walk back was worse than the whipping. I'd cry all the way back to her.

In her own way, she would take the switch from me and tell me, "I'm not gonna whip you. You have done whipped yourself."

But her way was tougher than the whipping, because you never knew if you were going to get whipped or not. It was tough. Funny, I never forgot that bush. Today, I still remember it. In today's world, they'd think that was child abuse—but it taught a lot of life lessons.

One of my life lessons that my grandmother taught me was to never run from a whipping. Her discipline was tough, but she always did it with fairness. Usually, it was I who caused the whipping. One time I did something I should not have done, and she was going to whip me—and I ran from her. I took off like a scalded dog, heart hammering, shoes slapping against the hard clay yard.

I was gone most of the afternoon. I had to go carry my papers, and then I was heading home. I did think about what was going to happen when I got home. As I entered the house, things seemed as usual. Supper was on the table, and Grandma was happy as usual. We sat down to eat supper. Nothing different.

I thought I got by with this one.

I finished my supper. Grandma said, "You need to do your homework and get your bath and get ready for bed."

"OK, Grandma," I said.

I was puzzled by this because I knew my grandma. You do not get by with anything with her. As the evening went along, I told my grandma I was going to bed.

She said, "Good night, son."

It was weird because I knew something was up. She was *too* nice. It was that quiet before the storm kind of nice.

I got into bed, turned my light out, and checked my alarm clock to get up at 4:30 a.m. to go to my paper route. I fell asleep fast. I was very tired from the day.

It was later in the night. I was buried in my feather tick bed asleep—warm, comfortable, dreaming about nothing in particular— then all of a sudden the bedroom light came on, and Grandma ripped the quilt off me and was whipping me with a switch.

It's tough getting whipped in your sleep.

I thought the world was ending. I was trying to dodge that switch with all my might, rolling and ducking, caught between sleep and survival. It seemed to last for hours, but it was just a minute or two.

Grandma started talking in a loud voice, with every swat: "Son, don't you ever run from me... ever again... from a whipping!"

And boy, I never did again.

As a little boy, my curiosity was running wild about that old Black man. My mind could not stop thinking about him—his world, his stories, everything he had been through in his life. The stories he had in his mind and heart. I know I would be back at the fence soon to watch him. I really wanted to get to know him.

As my day carried on, I had chores to do to finish up for the afternoon. I had to go throw my papers. My grandma told me she wanted some apples from the tree in the backyard, so I had to go to the back. I always liked doing the apple tree. I got to climb up the tree and shake it so the apples would fall to the ground and gather them up, and put them in the basket.

I loved my grandma's apple pies she baked—flaky crust, sweet cinnamon filling, hot out the oven with a scoop of melted butter on top. But that day, I was up in the tree, and I was looking out toward where the Black man lived. He didn't see me at first. I was on the limb just a-shaking it, and the apples were falling like crazy, thudding against the ground.

He was sitting on the back porch in his rocking chair. He was smiling and whittling something, slow and focused like the world didn't matter. Then he looked over at the tree and saw me in it.

He just started smiling and waving at me from the tree.

I hesitated. But then I just smiled and waved back. I felt good about it, but I didn't know if my grandma was watching me from the kitchen window. My eyes darted back toward the house, just in case.

The old man had something in his hand—a little object he had carved out of wood. I was far away, but I could see it in his hand, like a secret gift. He was waving it up in the air and pointing to the fence, like he wanted to give it to me.

Boy, was I CURIOUS.

The old Black man got up and started walking to the barbed wire fence. He set the object down and pointed to it, letting me know it was for me. I was still in the tree like a cat, perched up there with my heart thudding with excitement.

I wanted to come down and run to the border of the fence to get it.

I looked back at my house to see if my grandma was watching me, but I didn't see her. I climbed down from the tree, ran barefoot across the yard, and got to the fence to see what he gave me. I was so excited I nearly forgot to breathe.

When I got on the ground, I picked up a few apples to put at the fence for him. I was developing a friendship with him, but I was still unsure of him. Everybody was always telling me to stay away from colored people—it was a sign of that era.

He left the object at the fence and walked back to his porch, to his rocker.

When I finally got the courage to get to the fence, I saw what he had made for me. I picked it up underneath the fence. I had to stretch my short little arm way out on his side to retrieve it.

It was amazing.

He carved a little boy out of wood—it looked like me. It was the grandest thing I had ever seen. I waved at him and pointed to the ground to let him know I left him something, also. He smiled, and I saw him from his mimicked lips. He said, "Thank you."

As I headed back to the house, I put the little carving in my pocket. It was like gold to me. I know he worked hard on the carving. I was proud of it. But I knew eventually my grandma would see it, and I didn't know what she was going to say—and I didn't want a whipping, because she told me to stay away from him.

I never really felt afraid of him. He was a kind old man and smiled a lot. I knew people who are mean don't smile a lot. He was always happy, smiling and singing in his garden.

We really never talked to each other. We always just waved and smiled when we saw each other in the back. We just had a connection.

Grandma had supper on the table and hollered at me to come eat. I had to get my coal and wood in before nightfall. As I went in to eat, I had to wash my hands, and I put my little carving on the sink. As I finished up, I went to the kitchen to eat. I forgot I left my carving on the sink in the bathroom.

Uh oh. Grandma was in there. She came out to eat but didn't say anything.

Maybe she didn't see it, and it was still in the bathroom.

So I went back to get it—it was not there.

Grandma found it.

I headed back to the table to eat. There sat my little boy at my plate.

Grandma said, "Where did you get that?"

I couldn't lie. I had to tell the truth.

"Grandma, the old Black man made it and left it at the fence for me."

Nothing was said. It was stone quiet at first. The hesitation was killing me. I didn't know what was going to happen next.

Grandma just said, "It looks just like you. It's amazing. But don't you dare go past the fence. You can wave at him and smile, but don't dare go any further. We don't know that man or his family."

"Grandma, I gave him some of our apples. He was so kind and thankful."

"That's fine," my grandma said. "He did a good thing for you."

I felt so relieved, like a balloon, the air let out.

Time went on as the seasons were fixing to change, and I was always looking for the old man in the garden. Every day when I would get home from carrying papers, I would head out to the backyard, looking over the fence to watch my friend work his garden. I would leave apples at the fence every day for him.

A few days went by, and my apples were still at the fence. It worried me. The old man was not getting my apples. I did not know what to think. I missed my friend, seeing him in the garden. He always retrieved the apples I left him.

A couple of days later, I came home from my paper route. I looked over the fence at his house. There were a lot of people and cars there.

It scared me. I didn't know what was going on.

I was a little boy. I was confused.

Someone on the back porch saw me and started walking to the fence—another colored person. A man was waving at me, like not to run. He wanted to talk to me.

As he approached the fence, he said, "Hello. You must be my dad's little friend he talked about."

I said, "I'm not supposed to talk to colored people."

He said, "I understand, son. People are sometimes unkind and cruel."

I said, "I know. I don't understand things, and I don't question things."

"My dad passed away last night. He was 98 years old. He talked a lot about how he loved your apples."

My heart sank. I missed my friend.

I showed his son what he had made for me, and he smiled. He looked just like his dad. I told him I would never forget his dad.

And I haven't.

I was down for a number of days from the loss of my friend. Funny—we never talked to each other, but somehow we understood each other and knew the world with Black and white didn't mix. But we were friends, quietly.

In the '60s, racial inequality was so high, with all the riots and destruction in the cities. As a little boy, I never understood what skin color had to do with anything.

My grandma always told me, "God reads the heart, not the color of your skin."

But she still did not mix with colored people.

I was taught the same way growing up.

It was a difficult era.

I finally told my grandma that the old Black man died. My friend.

She already knew from the gossip in the neighborhood.

# CHAPTER 23
# A BLACK AND WHITE
# WORLD, WHY?

After the death of my friend, the old black man, I was troubled, as a young boy, wondering why we could not just get along. Even at my age, I couldn't understand why it had to be this way. I missed my old friend dearly. He'd been more than just an older man who lived by the fence—he'd been a confidant, someone who didn't care about the color of my skin, only about the kindness in my heart. Losing him felt like losing a part of myself, like something precious had slipped away forever.

The world around me wasn't any better. The rioting and looting were continuing in the city, and there was a constant unease in the air, a feeling that things just weren't right. The streets buzzed with whispers, rumors, and fears. Everyone seemed on edge, but they couldn't seem to figure out what to do about it. John F. Kennedy had just been assassinated, and the country was reeling from the shock. The world felt like it was unraveling, piece by piece, as if it was all slipping through our fingers.

At the same time, the desegregation of the school system had begun. I had heard the talk at the kitchen table, adults whispering about the changes, about the kids being bussed across town to different schools. And, sure enough, I was one of those kids. I was going to be bused across town to what everyone called "black town." I didn't know exactly what that meant, but I knew it scared me. I had never been to a school with black children before, and I didn't know how it would be. It was a fear I couldn't shake, but I tried to hide it from my grandmother, who was just as worried as I was. She fretted over everything, every little detail, her hands twisting at the apron she wore all day. She wanted to protect me from the world, but I told her I'd be okay. I told her I had been through so much already that it wouldn't be so bad.

As time passed, the tension in the air didn't ease. It seemed like everyone, even the grown folks, was uneasy. And maybe I wasn't old enough to understand it all, but I was tougher than I thought. Life had changed quickly for me, always moving fast, always twisting and turning. I had known nothing but change. Every day, something new seemed to come crashing down on me. But as fall arrived, it was time for me to face another change. It was time to board the bus across town, heading to that new school.

I remember standing at the bus stop, my stomach in knots. My nerves were like a storm churning in my gut. This was it. The first time I was sent across town, away from everything familiar. To me, it felt like an adventure—something new and exciting—but to everyone else, it was something they didn't like. The protests were everywhere. People were shouting, waving signs, causing a ruckus. The air was thick with anger and fear. But I just wanted to go to school. I thought about how the adults seemed to have all these issues, problems they didn't know how to fix. I wondered why it had to be like that. Why couldn't everyone just get along?

# JUST A SMALL TOWN SOUTHERN BOY

Looking back, I know that year was when the world took a dramatic tilt. The world, as I knew it, was never going to be the same.

The first day at the new school was something I'll never forget. The sight of black and white kids sitting in the same room felt strange to me. For the first time, I saw the separation disappear, but it wasn't something that felt right. After being in an all-white school for most of my life, this was something new, something different. It felt wrong and right at the same time. The air seemed to hum with tension, as if everyone was still figuring out how to make it work. I tried to see the good in everyone. I really did, especially after losing my dear black friend. I remembered how he'd treated me with such kindness, how he'd welcomed me like I was family. He was just a nice old man, and I missed him more than I could put into words.

The day went on without much trouble, and I thought maybe, just maybe, everything would be okay. I tried to let go of the fear for a little while. But then, it happened. We were in the lunchroom, sitting down to eat, when suddenly, out of nowhere, a fight broke out. Two black boys jumped a white boy, and in an instant, the room erupted into chaos. Panic spread like wildfire. Tables were turned over, and chairs flew through the air like baseballs. The noise was deafening—screaming, shouting, the sound of bodies crashing into one another. I hit the floor, crawling on my hands and knees, trying to get to safety. My heart was pounding so hard I thought it would explode right out of my chest. I wasn't sure where to go, but all I knew was that I had to get out of there.

The next thing I knew, police cars and tactical trucks were swarming the school. The air was filled with the sound of sirens, the screeching of tires, the loud churning of chaos. News media were everywhere—cameras flashing, microphones shoved in people's faces. It was like the whole world had descended on that lunchroom. The chaos felt like it would never end. Then came the tear gas. It stung my eyes and burned my throat like a thousand bees had flown straight into my lungs. I could barely breathe, my chest tight with every inhale.

I finally made it outside, my friend Terry right behind me. We didn't know where we were going, but we just wanted to get away. I didn't know my way home, and I didn't care. All I wanted was to get as far from that madness as I could.

"Now what?" I asked Terry, feeling a little lost.

"I know how to get to my house," he said, his voice steady. "Let's go."

I wasn't sure how far it was, but Terry seemed confident. We walked, the hot sun beating down on us, the humidity wrapping around us like a wet blanket. I could feel the sweat running down my back, soaking my shirt, but we didn't stop. We just kept moving, both of us too tired to think about anything except getting somewhere safe.

"Don't worry, Larry," Terry said. "We'll get there soon. It's only about four miles from here."

I couldn't even imagine how far that was, but I trusted Terry. He was a good kid, and he seemed to know what he was doing.

The closer we got to his house, the more my jaw dropped. I had never seen houses like this before. His neighborhood looked like something out of a movie—big houses, nice lawns, everything neat and perfect. I couldn't believe it. When we reached his house, I had to stop and stare.

"Is this where you live?" I asked, amazed.

"Yeah, right down the hill," Terry said. "I hope my mom's home. She's probably worried about me."

As we walked up the driveway, Terry's mom came running out the door, tears in her eyes. She grabbed Terry in a tight hug, holding him close, like she'd been scared for him. She looked at me, wiping away her tears.

"And who's this?" she asked.

"This is Larry," Terry said, introducing me. "We ran from school together."

She smiled and said, "Well, let's get you boys something to drink. I know you're both exhausted."

We went inside, and I was blown away. The house was nothing like anything I had ever seen before. It was a beautiful, two-story brick house, so nice it almost felt like a dream. I had never seen anything so clean, so perfect. Everything was neat and orderly, and the air inside was cool, a refreshing change from the oppressive heat outside.

I couldn't help myself. "How is your house so cool?" I asked.

Terry looked at me, a little confused. "It's air conditioning."

I felt my face flush. "What's that?"

"It's a heating and cooling system for the house, you just set it to heat or cool and turn it to where you want the temp to be." he explained.

I didn't want to sound stupid, but I couldn't help it. "You mean you don't have a coal stove or cut wood or nothing to stay warm ?" I asked.

Terry laughed. "What's that?"

I felt a lump in my throat. I had never been inside a house like this, never known anyone who lived like this. It made me feel small, like I didn't belong. But Terry didn't care. He just showed me how to adjust the dial on the wall, and I watched in awe as the room stayed perfectly cool. I had never seen anything like it.

His mom stayed quiet, just watching us, smiling but not saying much. She seemed to understand. I didn't want to seem rude, but I felt out of place. I had never realized how different our worlds were until that moment.

Terry's mom asked where I lived, and when I told her, she offered to drive me home. I didn't want her to. I didn't want her to see where I lived, didn't want her to think I was poor. It felt like a shame I couldn't explain.

We got in the car, and as we neared my house, I asked her to let me out a couple blocks away. I told her I'd walk the rest of the way. She insisted on driving me all the way, but I just couldn't let her see where I came from.

"Is this close enough?" she asked as we reached the intersection near my street.

I nodded. "Yeah, thank you for the ride."

I said goodbye to Terry, and as I walked away, I felt the weight of it all. It was more stressful for me than the riot. I had seen something that day, something I wasn't ready for.

When I got home, Grandma was on the front porch, sitting in her favorite swing. She had been worried, I could see it in her eyes. She had heard the news, knew about the riots, and she had been waiting for me, not knowing where I was.

She asked how I got home, and I told her about Terry's mom driving me after we ran from school. I didn't tell her the whole story. But she wasn't fooled.

She stared at me, her eyes narrowing. "I didn't see anyone drop you off," she said. "You walked in by yourself."

I froze. I didn't know how to respond. I could feel her gaze on me, reading me, seeing right through me.

"Okay, Larry Wayne," she said. "What's up?"

I knew I couldn't lie. Slowly, I told her the truth. I didn't want Terry's mom to see where I lived. I didn't want her to think we were poor.

Grandma paused for a long moment, staring at me, her face unreadable. Then, she spoke softly.

"You were ashamed where you lived?" she asked. "Why?"

I felt a knot in my stomach. I couldn't answer. I felt like I'd hurt her feelings, but she wasn't angry. She was just… sad.

She looked at me, her eyes softening. "Son, don't never be ashamed of where you live or where you're from. This is your home and your family. Everyone doesn't have what you have. There are people a lot worse off than you."

Her words sank deep into my soul. I felt my heart break a little. I felt like I had crushed her spirit, but she wasn't upset. She was just teaching me something I'd never forget.

"What is rich, Larry Wayne?" she asked. "Is it material things or love and a strong family? Remember, son, material things come and go, but love remains. All of life is an illusion."

That talk stayed with me, deep in my heart. From that day on, I never again felt ashamed of where I came from or what I had. I understood, for the first time, that love, family, and home were the true wealth of life.

# CHAPTER 24
# WHAT I HAVE LEARNED IN
# LIFE AT AN OLDER AGE

Being a product of the Baby Boomer generation was no fault of my own. It was just the way things happened. That generation- it was something special. There was a certain kind of magic about it, about growing up in that time. Born into a world that was full of change, full of promise. A blessing, I guess. When you're young, you don't really think about the bigger picture of what it means to be part of something larger, but as I've grown older, it's clearer to me now. Life, it's like a circle, and the path we walk often comes back to the people and things that shape us.

My mom was very young when she gave birth to me. I don't really remember her as much—she was a whisper of a figure in my early life—but she had me when she was just a girl herself. Life hadn't been kind to her either, and I guess that's part of the reason I ended up in foster care. Growing up in foster care from birth to age six wasn't easy, not for anyone, least of all a young boy trying to find his place in a world that seemed like it could be so cold. I went through three different homes in those six years, and I didn't belong to any of them. But what it did teach me was something I could hold onto for the rest of my life. It taught me to be strong. It taught me how to survive. Because when you're bounced around like that, you either sink or swim, and I was determined to swim.

I wasn't alone for long. I was fortunate, beyond measure, to have a grandmother who took me in when I was out of the foster system. She raised me. She loved me. And I never, ever took that for granted. My grandmother had raised fourteen kids of her own before me. Fourteen. That's not a number you just breeze past. And here I was, the fifteenth, just a boy with a lot of questions and not many answers. But she was a tough woman. The kind of woman who didn't back down from anything or anyone. Her generation, the one she came from, was built different. Stronger, in a way. It was in their bones. And she passed that strength down to me.

As I grew older, I started to see more and more the lessons she had taught me, even the ones I didn't understand at the time. Growing up without a father, it wasn't easy. I watched other kids with their moms and dads, with brothers and sisters, traveling, enjoying life, doing things together. It was a world I wasn't familiar with, a world I couldn't quite touch. All I knew was work. Work was what I had. My grandmother instilled that in me—work was the thing that could carry you through life, and if you worked hard enough, you could make something of yourself. She would always tell me, "Nobody's gonna take care of you but yourself."

She made sure I heard it loud and clear, like a constant hum in the background of my life. And you know what? She was right. The older I get, the more I realize that no one else can do it for you. You've got to take the reins. You've got to carry your own weight. I remember thinking that was harsh back then, but it was a hard truth, and a truth that has stuck with me.

# JUST A SMALL TOWN SOUTHERN BOY

I've always been the kind of person who listens to older folks. They've been through the fire and come out the other side. To me, that kind of wisdom was priceless. The way I looked at it, they didn't get to be old by being stupid. And, boy, there's a lot of truth in that. My grandmother lived to be 88 years old, and let me tell you, she lived a hard life. A real hard life, just like most of her generation. She worked from sunup to sundown and never complained. The kind of work that wore you down, but never broke you. I was lucky to have had her. Even though growing up wasn't always like champagne and strawberries, I wouldn't trade it for anything. She always told me, "One day, you'll understand," and, man, was she right. Looking back now, I get it.

I didn't have the best start in life, and I didn't have the luxury of a pretty, easy childhood. But you know what? A lot of people don't. It's a hard truth that some folks never come to terms with. But I've learned something along the way, and it's something I hope young folks will hear if they read this. Tough times don't last forever. They'll come, and they'll go. You just have to hold on through the storm. Never, ever give up. Life gets better. Stay strong. Hard times? They'll leave, and when they do, you'll be stronger for it.

I grew up in the '50s, '60s, and '70s. It wasn't an easy time for a boy with just a grandmother. We didn't have much, but we made do. It was a time when a lot of people struggled, but that struggle made us who we are today. Those were tough decades, but they shaped me, and in a strange way, I wouldn't change a thing. Because, through all the hardship, all the lessons learned the hard way, it made me stronger. It made me who I am today.

When I look at the younger generation today, it's different. Much different. It's a softer world now. Kids don't have to work like we did.

They grow up with more comfort, more convenience. It's an instant gratification world, where everything comes easy, where everything is just a click away. I respect the younger folks, don't get me wrong, but I wonder sometimes if they'll have the same kind of toughness that my generation did. I don't think there will be another generation like my grandmother's. Her generation had grit, had a strength that you don't see much these days.

Yes, growing up in the racially divided South was hard. Some things happened that were downright ugly, things that should never have happened. It's a sad chapter in our history, a chapter full of pain and regret. But here's what I've learned through all that pain: we're all just trying to make it in this world. No matter where we come from, no matter our color, our nationality, or our wealth. We're all just trying to survive and build a better life. The key, the real lesson I've learned through it all, is that you have to love and respect people, no matter their background, no matter what they look like or where they come from.

If you're a product of a single-parent home or if you grew up in foster care, don't lose heart. Stay strong. Life will teach you things that make you who you are, and it will make you a better person. Times will get better. You just have to hold on, stay steady, and keep moving forward. Like my grandmother always told me, "One day, you'll understand."

And now, looking back, I do understand. She was right all along. Life is tough, but it's worth it. And we get through it. Together, we get through it.

www.ingramcontent.com/pod-product-compliance
Lightning Source LLC
Chambersburg PA
CBHW051319120626
46547CB00015B/2310

*9 7 8 1 9 6 7 9 2 7 9 7 5 *